CODENAME INTREPID

THE SPYMASTER WHO CHANGED WORLD WAR II

ETHAN QUINN

© Copyright Ethan Quinn 2019. All rights reserved.

No part of this book may be reproduced in any form without permission in writing from the author. Reviewers may quote brief passages in reviews.

Polite Note for the Reader's Attention

Codename Intrepid has been written in UK English and certain words or phrases might vary from US English. This is except when loyalty to other languages and accents are deemed appropriate.

ISBN- 9781080768448

For Heidi and Nora

CONTENTS

William Stephenson.. 7

Chapter 1: Growing Up Through Adversity 9

Chapter 2: Flying With Prestige 18

Chapter 3: Peace Time Activities 26

Chapter 4: The Man Known As Intrepid 35

Chapter 5: An Intelligence Trailblazer 62

Chapter 6: Post-War Life 89

Chapter 7: Bill's Secret Agents 98

The Legacy of Intrepid 127

About Ethan Quinn 129

More Books by Ethan Quinn 130

Free Espionage Audiobook 132

William Stephenson

It's often said that a lie can travel halfway around the world while the truth is still putting on its shoes. While this adage often comes with nefarious connotations, in the case of Sir William Stephenson's lies – or more accurately, his withholding of the truth – is what allowed him to operate as one of the foremost espionage practitioners in history. As there is a lot of misinformation about the infamous Stephenson – and understandably so due to the role he played in history – it's important to bring together what can be verified to help create an account of one of the most important men in the history of the world. Stretching from his early life as an adopted child all of the way through to his later years, the story of William Stephenson is one of adventure and intrigue. The man known as 'Intrepid' had admirers who made up some of the most important and famous people of his time. From Winston Churchill to Roald Dahl, the influence of Intrepid knew almost no bounds.

Using as many verified sources as could possibly be found to piece together the most complete picture of this great man's life, this account of William Stephenson's life will delve into territory that has rarely been seen anywhere else. The story of Intrepid is one of incredible bravery combined with the ability to blend into any background. This is the story of The Quiet Canadian, William Stephenson.

Chapter 1: Growing Up Through Adversity

William Stephenson was born on the 23rd of January, 1897, in Winnipeg, Canada. Born William Samuel Clouston Stanger, he was the second child of William and Sarah Stanger. William was a Scottish immigrant, and Sarah was an Icelandic immigrant. Their first child, Gloria, had been born in December of 1895 but had tragically died by October 1896 while Sarah was pregnant with her second child, William, Jr. William would have two siblings: Maria, born in 1899, and Andrew, born in 1901. It was 1901 that brought on the second tragedy to hit the Stanger family.

William Stanger Senior was a hardworking man, working as a labourer, a carter, and a fireman throughout his years. This lifetime of working hard brought on muscular atrophy, and by November of 1901, just a few short months after

Andrew was born, William Senior succumbed to the illness which befell him.

The death of the elder William Stanger left Sarah Stanger in a quandary. She managed to get a job working as a cleaner for the local doctor, but it soon became clear to her that she did not have the financial capabilities to care for three young children. While she didn't want to give up any of her children, she felt that William would be the most appropriate as he was older than the other two and would cause any potential family far less trouble than a younger child. She spoke to her friend Kristen Stephenson regarding her options, and eventually, they decided that young William would be adopted by Kristen's family.

William Samuel Clouston Stanger then became William Samuel Stephenson. Unlike modern procedures, adoption was an incredibly complicated system back in its infancy. Due to this, William was never legally adopted by the Stephenson family, but he recognised them as his family from that moment on. There are no records of what happened to Sarah Stanger and the rest of the family after William was adopted, apart from one rumour that they moved to Chicago, possibly to make it easier on both William and Sarah. The prospect of having to see each other regularly would have been difficult for both of them and extremely confusing to William, who was just four years old at the time.

The Stangers and Stephensons were both part of the

Icelandic immigrant community within Winnipeg, meaning that culturally there was not a big change for William, or simply 'Bill,' as he came to be known, and his new father, Vigfus, also being a labourer meant that his new home life wasn't too dissimilar from his previous one. Kristina and Vigfus already had four children of their own – Gudlauger, Gudminder, Julianna, and Johinna. Julianna was the closest in age to him, being born in 1894. Gudlauger and Gudminder were twins and were born in 1891. The oldest of the Stephenson clan was Johinna, who was born in 1884.

This was a lot for the young Bill to take in, and he was mostly a very quiet child overall. The inclusion of a wide range of cousins and second cousins meant that Bill suddenly had a much larger family than what he had been accustomed to in his previous life. The larger family only served to compound his shyness, and this quiet nature was something that he carried with him throughout his life, despite the grandiose adventures he later became famous for.

Despite the upheaval and heartbreak that he had undergone so far in his life, Bill was a remarkable child. Others quickly learned that Bill possessed an *eidetic memory*, colloquially referred to as a *photographic memory*. As a party trick, family members would ask Bill to leave the room, and while he was outside, ask him to list the items that were in the room. Unsurprisingly to his family, Bill would carry out this request with almost supernatural accuracy. However, despite this gifted ability, Bill struggled with his early studies and didn't even manage to get all of the way through school. It wasn't that he was unable to carry out what was required of him academically, but the financial issues within the house meant that Bill had to leave at the end of the sixth grade. It wasn't because the school cost money; it was so that Bill could find a job and help out with his family's financial burdens. Therefore, at the age of twelve, Bill Stephenson found himself working for the local lumber yard. It may have been a waste of his talents, but the Stephenson household was not a rich one and the extra money that he brought in made sure that the bills were paid on time and everyone ate properly.

The construction of a train line had led to several factories relocating to Winnipeg, bringing with them an abundance of work for those who sought it. However, this influx of industry brought with it its own issues. A significant number of brothels popped up, due in large part to the sheer number of working men now frequenting the area. This led to Winnipeg eventually gaining a reputation for being seedy and unwholesome.

Quite often, brothel business would be conducted in plain view in the streets. Parents ceased sending their children to school in the area due to its ever-worsening reputation. This then led to a political battle in 1910 between politicians and the church, with politicians eventually claiming victory, therefore allowing brothels to remain in business in Winnipeg for the foreseeable future.

It didn't take long for Bill to advance his career. Very soon, he began delivering telegrams for the local telegraph company, a job that brought a small pay rise and increase in responsibility. It was here that his presence in many different parts of Winnipeg throughout the day, combined with his eidetic memory, allowed Bill to have a part in the capture of a dangerous criminal.

On December the 3rd, 1913, the village of Plum Coulee in Manitoba had its usually-tranquil nature shattered to pieces by a violent crime. A bank manager at a local branch was shot and killed during an armed robbery by a single perpetrator. The culprit used a disguise, but he had made a fatal error when leaving the scene of the crime. He left a distinctive watch in the getaway car, and it was eventually traced back to a man named John Krafchenko.

Krafchenko was a career criminal and someone who romanticised the art of theft. He had recently been released from prison, where he had served two years for a similar crime and had been working in Winnipeg under a pseudonym. As soon as Krafchenko was confirmed as a suspect, his photograph and description were sent across the whole of Canada and even spread into the northern territories of the United States. It took just eight days for John Krafchenko to be captured, and it was sixteen-year-old Bill Stephenson who had notified the police of the criminal's whereabouts.

Bill's job delivering telegrams meant that he spent all day riding around the city on his bicycle. He had seen the photo of the wanted man, and it was therefore seared into his memory the moment he laid eyes on it. When he happened to stumble upon Krafchenko while doing his rounds, Bill instantly notified the police. While this was not reported in the newspaper for fear of reprisals from Krafchenko's friends on the outside, people within the Icelandic community who resided in Winnipeg were well aware that it was one of their own who had helped catch this dangerous criminal. It was fortunate that the information was never publicly released because Krafchenko ended up escaping from his prison cell only a few weeks later. It took eight days for him to be recaptured, and fortunately for young Bill, he had remained safe the whole time. Krafchenko was tried for murder and robbery and sentenced to death by hanging. On the 9th of July, 1914, John Krafchenko was hanged, marking the first time that remaining under a veil of secrecy would benefit Bill Stephenson. And of course, it wouldn't be the last.

Later that year, tensions between opposing factions of the world came to a head, resulting in the outbreak of World War 1. Bill continued to work for the telegraph company as war operations grew, but due to his athletic nature and build – partly owing to his spending twelve hours a day riding a bicycle – Bill considered offering his services to his country.

In January of 1916, Bill enlisted in the Winnipeg Light Infantry. However, despite his constant bike riding and general fitness levels, he was given a cause for unfitness and was only passed as a bugler. As such, he was sent out to train on the outskirts of Winnipeg. There, he sent a postcard to Gudlauger Stephenson's son, Harold, complaining about the cold conditions.

It took until July for Bill to be posted to somewhere abroad. On the 6th of July, he set sail for England. Once again, he sent Harold a postcard, this time just letting him know he had arrived at his destination safely – although he didn't give any details due to the heightened levels of secrecy that were in place during the war. While in England, Stephenson performed his duties to a high level and was transferred to the 17th battalion; he had hardly been in England for long enough to empty his rucksack before he was travelling to yet another country. This time he was sent to France.

While there, Stephenson suffered his first serious war injury. He was wounded by a French soldier within the first week and also fell victim to an attack of chemical warfare. Officials then sent him back to England to recover before the end of July.

In less than one month, Bill had travelled to two brand-new countries, been wounded and gassed, and then been sent back to the first country he'd travelled to. It was a back and forth lifestyle that he hadn't expected when he signed up. Bill was sent to Oxford to fully recover, which took him over a year, and during this time, he dedicated himself to bettering himself as a soldier and a man. He enrolled in courses about flight theory, navigation, and combustion engines. Bill wasn't just preparing himself for what might come next in the war; he was readying himself for what might come after the war. He wanted to be a more attractive proposition to employers when the war was over, and his eidetic memory was perfectly suited to learning the information he needed to do so. While he was consuming every piece of information that he could about flying and aviation, he also set a record time for wireless communication. He showed his worth to everyone around him, ensuring that everyone there took notice of the slight young lad who had an incredible work ethic and a faultless memory. Not only did he focus on making his mind an improved tool, he also trained his body. Bill pursued canoeing, weaponry discipline, and all manner of physical exertions. He intended to be ready next time he was out in the field – he had no intention of falling victim to an opposing soldier again.

The army quickly noticed the vast array of skills of their young soldier and soon put him to work carrying out some instruction. There is also a possibility that during this time Bill met with William Donovan, who would later become the head of America's Office of Strategic Services as well as play an important part in Bill's life story. Although Donovan himself disputes this and says that they didn't meet until 1940 at the earliest, there is a letter home to his wife where he talks about meeting a Canadian while in London. It is possible that the two met, but as Bill wasn't a prominent figure at this point, it may have just slipped Donovan's mind, and he didn't realise that he had indeed come into contact with the notorious Bill Stephenson.

The army began to take notice of Bill's hard work and subsequent improvement. By September of 1916, he had been promoted from soldier to an acting sergeant, subsequently being promoted to full sergeant. Bill was ecstatic with the news, realising now that his hard work had already begun to pay off, even at the mere age of nineteen. He was delighted and wanted to tell his confidant, Harold, but he knew that doing so could jeopardise his newfound position. It would have to wait. He continued working hard and attempted to make sure that his new skills would be put to good use. By 1917, his hard work finally paid off, and once again he was transferred to a new division. He would be taking up a position in the Royal Flying Corps.

Chapter 2: Flying With Prestige

It was in April of 1917 that Bill Stephenson joined the Cadet Wing of the Royal Flying Corps. His hard work meant that despite being a relatively short man, standing at a mere five foot, five inches tall, he had still managed to work his way up to a heralded position as a potential pilot. He initially joined in the Cadet Wing of the Royal Flying Corps, and by February of 1918, he had managed to achieve his pilot's license and was subsequently deployed to France.

Once on French soil, Bill joined up with the 73rd Squadron. Here, he was given the once-over by the orderly officer – a brash and outspoken Canadian by the name of Thomas Drew-Brook.

Drew-Brook took one glance at the young Stephenson and immediately decided that he wasn't up to the standards of the 73rd Squadron. Bill was still quite pale and thin as he hadn't fully recovered from the effects of the gas attack he suffered the last time he was in France, and Drew-Brook believed this was also taking its toll on his physical and mental well-being. Drew-Brook then went to the Flight Commander for the 73rd Squadron and recommended that Bill Stephenson be transferred to A Flight, but the suggestion was ignored, and Bill was to remain a part of the 73rd Squadron. While Drew-Brook hadn't been impressed by Bill Stephenson at first, the two men would eventually make firm friends. Bill was determined to begin pushing himself so that he could become the advanced pilot he now had aspirations of becoming.

His first decision that came from pushing himself was to taking up various contact sports, the most prominent being boxing. Due to his diminutive stature – even in the early 20th Century, 5'5" was considered to be short – combined with his thin figure from the gas attack, Bill first started boxing at Featherweight level. This was something that he would come to deny later in life, claiming that he had boxed at Lightweight, perhaps as a way to brush over his shortcomings. However, the records from the Inter-Allied Games in Amiens show that Bill Stephenson had previously won the Featherweight title. Perhaps if he hadn't been such a successful Featherweight boxer, no one would have ever known that his claims of boxing at Lightweight weren't true.

During his boxing career, Bill Stephenson made friends

with the future Heavyweight Champion of the World, Gene Tunney. He actually used his friendship with Tunney in later years to help him achieve various goals, and Tunney never had a bad word to say about Stephenson and even complimented his boxing skills in a radio interview in the 1960s. By March of 1918, Bill Stephenson was one of the most highly regarded fighter pilots in the whole of the 73rd Squadron. According to Drew-Brook, Stephenson had been shot down by two German fighters. Rather than making his way to the medical room to receive attention, Bill was so furious that he ran straight to another fighter plane and made his way to the sky to enact revenge. Drew-Brook heard the report come through that the two German fighters had been shot down and that Stephenson was returning to base. This was the beginning of the legend of Bill Stephenson as a fighter pilot.

While there are no exact records of how many fighters Bill shot down before he was shot down himself and captured, the lowest number suggested is 18 fighters, with the highest being 26 fighters and two weather balloons. Whichever record is the truth, or whether it is actually somewhere in between, it was a highly impressive record that led to Stephenson being classed as one of the best fighter pilots the 73rd Squadron had.

It was July 28, 1918 that Bill Stephenson was shot down and captured. He had been flying a solo mission across enemy lines because the usual scout patrol had been cancelled due to adverse weather conditions. Just under five miles inside the

German lines, Bill spotted a French reconnaissance plane being attacked by seven German Fokkers. Stephenson instantly initiated combat with his machine. He managed to start by shooting down the leader of the Fokker squadron. As the Fokker became engulfed in flames and spiralled towards the ground, Stephenson had already strafed into the clouds to gain some measure of camouflage. By using his altitude as a strategic tool to even up the odds – despite having shot down the leader of the Fokker biplanes, Bill was still outnumbered – he managed to turn what should have been a massacre into a prolonged aerial dogfight. He shot down another plane as well as causing a third plane to stall and fall from the sky with his incredible manoeuvres. It's unknown exactly what happened to Bill after he felled his third Fokker, but something caused his plane to fall into a nose-dive. The pilot of the French recon plane later claimed that he thought he saw gunfire hit his engine, thus potentially causing the nose-dive, but he also claimed he saw it out of the corner of his eye and could not be absolutely certain of what happened.

What is known is that once Bill crashed his plane in front of the German lines, he climbed out of his vehicle and crawled away but was shot in the leg before being captured by German forces. As there were no parachutes on the Allied planes at the time, there was zero opportunity for Bill to bail out before his plane reached German territory. Eyewitnesses later claimed that Bill Stephenson attempted to crawl away from the plane, but Bill himself claimed that the last thing he remembered was crashing in front of the German lines. While the true course of events remains unknown, the French Government wasted no time in awarding him the Croix de Guerre Avec Palme – an award given to soldiers or units who distinguished themselves with acts of bravery during combat. Bill had certainly done this, although at the time he wasn't even aware that he had been awarded the honour due to his captivity.

Bill survived his leg wound, discovering that he had been shot twice. It isn't known if he was shot twice while attempting to escape or whether the bullets entered his flesh during his aerial battle with German forces.

He was kept captive in Holzminden, a prisoner-of-war camp the Germans used exclusively for British and British Empire officers. Meaning being locked up in solitude for weeks on end, imprisonment inside opposing territory was a torturous experience. Not only did he expect death to come ripping by at any given moment, but the isolation pushed him to the brink of madness. He had little contact with fellow inmates, so he could not even while away his hours with fellow British officers. Bill's arduous experience only worsened the longer he was imprisoned. He began to feel like his entire war effort had been in vain. He had dedicated the past few years wholly to the pursuit of becoming the best soldier and pilot in Britain, only for his efforts to be sabotaged at one of the first hurdles.

Even while a prisoner of war, Bill still attempted to stage his own resistance against the enemy and took to stealing from the guards where he could. These actions didn't endear him to all the other prisoners as Bill had no qualms about stealing from them, too, if they died, providing he could come within close proximity of them.

Although the Germans generally treated the officers better than other prisoners of war, this didn't mean they had a life of luxury, either. Dreadful crimes against humanity took place inside the walls of Holzminden, with prisoners even being killed with bayonets if the camp Kommandant felt that it was justified. It was actually described as the worst camp in Germany by post-war researchers, but despite the horrors that lay within, Bill still managed to spend his time stealing to great effect.

A short while after Bill had been captured, Thomas Drew-Brook suffered a similar fate, although his physical condition was much worse than Bill's, and he had to spend some time in the camp infirmary. As soon as he was able to, Bill visited his friend in the hospital. While there, and sure that no one was listening, Bill began to tell Thomas all about his kleptomaniacal tendencies. He informed him of everything that he had stolen from the various guards at the camp, but there was one thing of which he was particularly proud. Bill had managed to steal a can opener from the food store. This can opener seemingly held no great importance to Thomas when Bill showed it to him, but Bill had a sharp business head on his shoulders, and he knew just how significant it was. The Germans had patented the can opener in 1915, but before they were able to patent it in other countries, the war had broken out. Bill was aware of this, and he intended to escape from the camp and patent the can opener in as many countries as he could.

Bill saw this as a double-edged sword. Firstly, it would be an excellent business decision as it would allow Bill to make money with very little effort. Secondly, it would be striking a blow at the Germans, the people who had not only started a war but had also imprisoned him and treated him in such an inhumane fashion. Thomas was impressed with his friend's sharp mind and promised to keep the information to himself.

It didn't take Bill long to make good on his promise to escape. While there are no records of exactly when he managed to flee the walls of Holzminden, it is possible that he managed to escape during the large-scale jailbreak in 1918. Twenty-nine officers scaled the borders of the camp and escaped to freedom, but it is not known for sure if Bill was one of the men. All that is known is that Bill managed to get back to Canada – more specifically, in Winnipeg with his parents – by 1919, so it must have been near to the end of the war when he managed to escape.

Bill's experience in the prisoner-of-war camp had a profound effect on him for many years, so much so that he kept a picture of the camp Kommandant that he had stolen long after the war had finished. It wasn't just the bad times that affected him, however. Bill had managed to attain the rank of Captain by the end of the war, hence why he had been kept in an officers' camp during his imprisonment, and he won more medals than just the Croix de Guerre Avec Palme that the French had awarded him. He was also awarded a Military Cross and Distinguished Flying Cross. Both of these were awarded for his flying prowess and the amount of damage he managed to cause to the enemy. Bill was also successful in smuggling the can opener back to Canada with him. He got in touch with a friend he had made before the war, Charles Russell, and they started a company called Franco-British Supply. It was through this company that they patented the can opener, rebranding it as the 'Kleen Kut'. This was because can openers from this period were on the whole inefficient and messy. The Kleen Kut was not. It smoothly opened cans and was far superior to the can openers of the time, which was perhaps why Bill was so intent on smuggling it out with him when he escaped. This was the start of Bill's life as a businessman, which was how he spent his life between the two World Wars.

Chapter 3: Peace Time Activities

Bill and Charles were intent on expanding their business. They began to act as agents for hardware companies that had products in the same vein as their Kleen Kut. Anything that carried out tasks in an improved manner to the tools of the day was something that they were happy to get behind. They moved into cutlery and even car parts. The success of the Kleen Kut had given Bill and Charles a good name, and they used this to make money from a whole host of other products. Bill even began trying his hand at inventing himself. He invented an innovative new mousetrap, which he took around different hardware supply shops until he finally managed to convince someone to sell it in their store. The grass didn't grow under Bill's feet because he was never still for long. Bill had new ideas pop into his head daily, which he often blindly pursued without any real plan as to where his efforts were headed. It wasn't that he was greedy and chased financial stability – it was that the ideas seemed to come so effortlessly to him that he felt it a waste not to indulge them.

Bill relocated to a more affluent area of Winnipeg during 1919, and it was in the September of that year that he first met a man who would have a large part to play in his later life: The Prince of Wales, who was to be the future king and also future Duke of Windsor. Just like his meeting with William Donovan, neither man knew the significance of their meeting at this point.

By 1921, Bill and Charles felt that they were ready to make the next step with their business. They went about soliciting investment capital from their family and friends and took the step of setting up a fully registered company. By February of 1921, they had managed to gain enough capital, and their new company, Stephenson-Russell Limited, was fully incorporated. This time, it wasn't just a two-man band like their previous incarnation. Instead, they chose to employ multiple directors to oversee their business venture – people with expertise in other areas, specifically the areas that Bill and Charles were weak in. They brought a broker and two lawyers on board as directors, and from the initial three-hundred share offering, each new director was given one free share. The share capital for the new company was set at $30,000 Canadian, meaning that each share was worth $100 individually, which would have an inflated value of $1,400 in today's economy. The two young entrepreneurs spent a lot of their time and effort attempting to make their business work. However, they hadn't accounted for the fact that Canada was struggling amid a recession.

Post-war Canada wasn't a good place to set up a business. The expansion that Bill and Charles undertook, combined with the poor level of business, meant that they struggled to find any success. A hardware store that they set up went out of business because there just wasn't enough custom. Even the can opener that Bill had smuggled from the POW camp didn't sell. It wasn't that the product wasn't good enough – it was, in fact, a revolutionary product and was the best can opener on the market by a considerable margin. The issue was that no one had the money to buy their can opener, leaving them with an incredible product that no one could afford to buy. If they had sold it cheaper, they would have taken a loss. They were stuck between a rock and a hard place.

By August of 1922, Stephenson-Russell Limited filed for bankruptcy. They had been unable to pay their taxes or their rent. Of the 97 creditors that they had, only 11 of them received the money owed to them; the rest received just 4.5% of what they were owed.

Bill didn't hang around in Winnipeg for long after the bankruptcy of his company. He left for England as soon as he could. There were several reasons for this. Firstly, he had borrowed a lot of money from family and friends to set up the company. It wasn't the creditors in the form of businesses that he was worried about, but the family and friends as well as the wider Icelandic community that he owed money to. He felt that he would never be able to get out from under the spectre of that debt, and he would either spend his life working to pay it off, or physical harm would be dealt out to him. Secondly, he was also worried that there might be a warrant out for his arrest. Some of the activities that Bill had carried out while trying to make a success of his company had been a little bit close to the knuckle in terms of legality. There had been a suspicious fire while Bill had been in charge of the business during a time when Charles had been on the road attempting to drum up business. While there is no record of Bill being the culprit, there were a lot of fingers pointed at Bill, possibly as some form of insurance scam to try and cover their debts. Because of all of this trouble, and because he was just looking for a fresh start, England was to be his destination.

It is thought that Bill actually started travelling to England before the bankruptcy had even been confirmed. By June 1922, he had already stopped in on his friend Thomas Drew-Brook in Toronto, albeit for a short time, and was well on his way to England. Once he made it there, he met up with a friend, Charles Farquhar. He stayed with Farquhar for a while when he first got there, and as soon as he was able, he set up his company again. Stephenson-Russell was reborn in London during 1922. While he had been working in Canada, Bill had gained some insight into how radios were manufactured. He felt that this was an area that would undergo a lot of growth over the next few years and decided to focus his efforts on getting his foot through the door of radio manufacture and distribution. He went about this with a different method to his Canadian business practices. Instead of attempting to compete with already established companies, Bill invested in companies that were already working within the industry. He didn't just invest in companies that manufactured and distributed radios, either; Bill invested in companies that carried out research, as well.

It was through the research-centric companies that Bill met and started working with T. Thorne Baker. Baker was an expert in photo-telegraphy. This was a relatively new field and involved the transmission of images via radio. Baker had invented a way to send photos over telephone lines and had been working on a way to use wireless technology to transmit photographs. Bill began working on the project with Baker. Even though Bill had very little experience working with electronics, he still managed to be very useful to Baker. Baker had been using selenium to convert light into electric currents, but the process was far too slow to be of any real use to anyone. Somehow Bill managed to devise a light-sensitive device that could carry out the process at a much faster rate. Bill realised that if he could somehow speed up the process even further, then the possibilities were endless. Although Bill did not have a hand in the invention of television, the technology that he developed did come as a precursor to the eventual technology that would bring television to the mass market.

Bill had made his mark on the radio and wireless industry, and by August of 1923, just over a year after he had landed in England, he was made the managing director of two separate companies, one based in electronics and the other based in radio. Together, they worked on radios, wireless technology, and X-rays.

Bill continued his research work and was successful in transmitting photos by wireless for *The Daily Mail*. In the summer of 1923, Bill returned to Canada for an exhibition in Toronto. While there, he met up with Charles Russell, who returned to England with Bill.

On their journey back to England, Bill and Charles struck up a rapport with two ladies on their boat. They engaged in deep conversation for the majority of the journey, discovering that the ladies were sisters and their family were tobacco growers in Tennessee.

Bill fell head over heels for one of the young ladies, named Mary French Simmons, and the two became inseparable after their ship docked in England. It wasn't long before the pair were married.

Their wedding took place in August of 1924. Such was the prominence of Bill and Mary, their marriage was even featured in *The New York Times*, with Bill being described as a scientist who had invented a device to send photographs by radio. Bill had managed to leave behind his past failures in Canada and was earning both money and reputation overseas. Charles eventually married Mary's sister, and the two men remained close friends.

Bill continued to be a success in England. He patented the method of sending photographs by wireless, eventually passing the million-pound profit mark. He achieved this impressive milestone before the age of 30, and when taking into account that £1,000,000 would be worth £14,000,000 today, it makes it all the more impressive. Bill continued to expand his horizons, and in 1925 he set up a holding company, named Stephenson Taylor, with another Canadian. By the end of the 1920s, the company had a name change, to Pacific Trust, and began scouring the globe for investment opportunities. Pacific Trust began to undertake work all over the world, building residential areas, bridges, and even aircraft. Bill just kept moving forward. By the 1930s, he controlled a cement company, one of the largest in England, and a steel company that was involved in the manufacture of the vast majority of the car bodies made in England. Bill was even involved in building an apartment block that contained central heating, a rarity for most houses at the time, let alone an apartment block.

Bill even started to get involved in the world of film. He set up production companies in the early 1930s, and by 1934, seven films were produced by Bill's company. His reach and influence were starting to become vital aspects of his life. Not only was he a man involved with some of the largest companies in England, but his social circle increased to include some of the most important people in the country – most notably, a politician named Winston Churchill. This was a relationship that would take on a much more crucial role in the not-too-distant future.

Bill's work with his many businesses meant that he travelled all around the world. He was the leader of a mission to Asia and Africa, where his technical expertise was used to attempt to utilise the natural resources that were abundant on both continents. It also took Bill to Germany, where he first became aware of the rise of Adolf Hitler. It was during one of his trips to Germany that he became worried about the direction that the country was taking and started creating reports to take back with him to give to his politician friends.

Despite Bill's success in business, his family back in Canada was not so successful. His sister Julianna had died in 1928, just four years after she had visited Bill. She had fallen ill during the trip back from England and had never fully recovered from the illness, although some family members still believe that Bill almost cutting off the family had upset her to such a degree that it killed her. His father died in 1937, and his mother followed not long after, in 1940. Perhaps being an adopted son meant that Bill didn't feel much loyalty to his family, but he never visited them after he fled Winnipeg to move to England, and the only contact that any of his family had with him was when Julianna came to visit in 1924. Bill continued to have a great deal of success in business for the remainder of the 1930s, but there was one thing that stood to change all that. On the 1st of September 1939, Germany invaded Poland. This would be the beginning of the Second World War.

Chapter 4: The Man Known As Intrepid

Even though war didn't break out until 1939, Bill had been involved in the English preparations for the outbreak of war. England had been aware of what Hitler was doing for quite some time, and Bill played a large part in collating the information that they had.

Despite moving up in the world, in terms of both money and his social circle, Bill hadn't become a lazy or conceited person. He had grown up with nothing. Such was the extent of how poor his family was that he had been given away to a family friend when he was a young boy. He knew the importance of hard work and made sure that he kept his work ethic throughout his life, no matter what task he was undertaking.

Bill had become involved in the process of intelligence at

some point during the 1930s. The precise date isn't known, but during the 30s, all of Bill's records were hidden. All of the company records that had his name were either taken into government files or completely redacted. His history before the mid-1930s was almost entirely wiped.

While the exact details of how Bill became a vital part of the wartime cog are lost to the mists of time, it is thought that one of his high society friends first introduced him to the head of Britain's Secret Intelligence Service, Stewart Menzies. Bill had been getting the raw materials for his steel company from Sweden, which incidentally was the same place that Ralph Glyn's company got their raw materials. Glyn was a Conservative MP and a friend of Menzies. This is the most probable link between the two men, as well as being how Menzies himself claimed the two met, although Bill never made known his version of how they met.

It is believed that Bill made his first tentative steps into the world of espionage during the construction of the Earl's Court Exhibition building. There is no record of who owned the building. However, there is a record of bankruptcy. Bill was one of the directors listed on this record along with Ralph Glyn and Maurice Bonham Carter, who was a close friend of Winston Churchill. It was during 1936 that this building was first brought into prominence, so this is most likely the year that Bill first started to be a major figure in the intelligence world. One of the biggest factors that led to his inroads in the war effort was his business interests. Due to Britain engaging on a course of rearmament, there was a shortage of steel. Because Bill was involved in the steel and aircraft industries, his knowledge of this situation was likely to be better than most.

It was during 1936 that Bill really started to lay the groundwork for his future position in the intelligence service during the war. Winston Churchill was not in power at the time, but he was still an important figure within Westminster, especially for the information that he was providing. Most of that information was coming from Bill. He had seen that the Germans were violating the Treaty of Versailles. Hitler had built his platform on reneging on the Treaty of Versailles – the Nazi Party had called the previous government who had signed it the 'November Criminals' – but despite this obvious disdain for the treaty in their own party manifesto, they had still attempted to hide what they were doing. Bill saw this when he travelled to Germany, and he began relaying this information to Churchill. The Germans had started to build up their armed forces again and had even managed to spend £800,000,000 on their military, although this money was hidden through several creative accounting methods. By passing this information to Churchill, Bill gave him something solid to take back to Parliament. It was vital that this information was handed over as soon as possible because the government at the time either didn't believe the suspicions of the MPs or didn't care about them. This meant that there was almost a rebellion within Parliament, while MPs outside of the acting government were building up an intelligence dossier to ensure that in the likely event of war, they would be as prepared as possible.

The information that Bill provided was wide-ranging, and although it was in 1936 that he was passing his reports over, he had actually started collating it as early as 1933. He witnessed the Nazis burning books in 1933; in 1934 he found out about a lot of Nazi strategies after meeting with their military officials, and in 1935 he actually met with Nazi leaders and had one stay with him. He managed to do this through having a lot of his personal history erased. He was seen as a Canadian, not an Englishman. With his history redacted, he portrayed himself as someone who admired Nazi Germany. This allowed him unprecedented access to them without arousing an ounce of suspicion. Even though Bill hadn't even been approached to act as a spy, he had personally decided to go through security measures to ensure both his safety and his ability to find out as much information as possible. It could be said that Bill Stephenson was something of a natural spy.

It was through a man named Desmond Morton that Bill passed his first reports. It's thought that he gave information to Morton in 1934, a full two years before he started providing

Churchill with information. In a somewhat ironic twist, Morton passed on all reports that he received to Churchill. So despite not being in direct contact with him until 1936, Bill was indirectly feeding him information in 1934. All of this came because they shared a mutual distrust of Nazi Germany. In November of 1934, Winston Churchill used the information that he had collated through his numerous sources to warn Parliament of the impending German threat. Despite being warned about their rearmament, parliament was surprisingly unsupportive. Therefore, the process of rearming Britain was incredibly slow.

The information that MI6 had about the Nazi threat tended to agree with the information that Churchill had collected. According to FW Winterbotham, who was working within MI6 during this time, their information tallied up almost exactly to that which Churchill was gathering. There were a number of times that Churchill would speak in parliament about the German threat, and the Prime Minister at the time, Stanley Baldwin, would claim that he had no information on the subject. According to Winterbotham, this was an outright lie as he had been briefed on this several times. That the information that Bill Stephenson had been able to collect matched up to that which MI6 had collected, one of the top intelligence agencies in the world, was remarkable. It also showed that he had a talent for espionage.

By May 1935, Baldwin had finally started to agree with what Churchill had been saying for the previous six months. Baldwin started to claim that he had been misled on the subject, which was why he had been brushing off Churchill's claims. MI6, of course, denied that he had been misled and thought that he was just attempting to shift the blame. By July, Britain started the process of rearming with aplomb, but by this point, they were well behind the German rearmament. Baldwin had claimed that the Germans were building 100 planes per year. The actual figure was closer to 150 each month. This meant that the Germans were actually building almost 18 times as many planes as Baldwin publicly claimed they were. It wasn't just politicians who were feeding this line either. The media did, too. All too often the media fed the public the line that the claims about the Germans were overblown. The motivation to lie about this has never been found out. It could have been overconfidence; it could have been that someone within the cabinet sympathised with the Nazis, or it could have just been sheer incompetence. We will likely never know. What we do know is that Britain's inaction certainly played a large part in how quickly the Germans were able to escalate and begin carrying out their plan.

Even though Bill was providing vital information to Churchill directly as early as 1936, he still wasn't officially brought into the fold until 1938, at the earliest. In fact, there is even evidence to show that before Bill was brought in officially, he had planned to assassinate Hitler. Because he was known as someone who admired the Nazis, he knew that it would be possible for him to get into the country with relative ease. Bill's plan was to use a sniper rifle to kill Hitler at one of his rallies. He knew that it would be a suicide mission, but he was also willing to carry it out for the greater good of the world. Bill took his plan to the Secret Service, but the foreign secretary at the time decided that the plan shouldn't take place. He was still of the opinion that Hitler and the Nazis could be negotiated with.

Bill had also been part of a plan to stop the transportation of iron ore from Sweden to Germany. This plan was stopped at the last minute by the King of Sweden. Ironically, the iron ore in Sweden led to Germany making inroads in Scandinavia soon after war broke out. They invaded Norway and Denmark to surround Sweden and protect the iron ore, which by this point the Allied forces had realised was an important part of the German rearmament process. If Bill had been allowed to carry out this plan, then it is possible that war could have been averted as the Germans wouldn't have been able to rearm themselves at such a fast rate.

The Germans started invading neighbouring countries as early as 1936. At first, this was overlooked by several politicians because they were taking back land they had lost in the First World War. While they were not pleased about it, they were also not sufficiently upset to start another war. By 1938, they had invaded the Rhineland, Austria, and Czechoslovakia. It was at this point that Bill finally met up with Churchill to discuss the pressing German problem. A mutual friend, Fred Leathers, whom Bill knew from the cement industry, invited Bill to lunch with Churchill as he knew that Bill had strong opinions on the way the Germans were going about their business. He also knew that Bill had been secretly providing a number of people within the government with information for some years now. Both men agreed that the Germans were dangerous and that Britain was massively unprepared to deal with the prospect of war. They agreed to stay in close contact in order for Churchill to use Bill's knowledge to help formulate a plan.

By the time war broke out in September of 1939, the world was in turmoil. Several countries were engaged in hostilities with each other, and the Germans were using this to their advantage. They knew that the problems that many of the Allied countries were facing only made their position stronger. The American president, Franklin Roosevelt, was distressed by the actions of Germany. The Germans had claimed their initial invasions were them carrying out their rights to have colonies. Roosevelt felt differently – he thought that the Nazis had committed war crimes. His ambassador to England felt differently. He advised the president against joining in with the war. He told President Roosevelt that joining in with the war would be fruitless as not only were the Allies likely to lose, but they also expected to lose. The ambassador felt that Britain was a lost cause and could even end up under Nazi rule. While the President didn't engage with the war, he did begin privately contacting Winston Churchill, a man who was gaining more influence within Parliament as well as being someone he trusted.

This correspondence with Churchill led to Roosevelt being worried about the lack of intelligence agencies in the United States. They had no form of intelligence at this point. Therefore, Roosevelt wrote to Churchill asking for his help in setting up an intelligence agency. Churchill's advisors chose the man that they thought best for the job: Bill Stephenson.

There were a large number of reasons why Bill was chosen to be the man to set up an American intelligence network, but the main one was that his information had been so accurate. Bill had managed to collect information that was almost identical to the information that MI6 had been able to collect. One man had collected the same information as the best intelligence agency in the world. This meant that the people within Churchill's inner circle recognised Bill as a man with incredible talents within the field of espionage. They also thought that he would be well suited to report back to the British Intelligence Agency with any relevant information from America. It was the perfect job for Bill and one that he would be able to carry out with relative ease.

Another reason that Bill was chosen rather than someone from the British Intelligence Agency was that there was a suspicion that MI5 and MI6 had Nazi sympathies. There were rumours that the British Prime Minister at the time, Neville Chamberlain, had made a deal with Hitler in 1938. This deal was said to be that the Germans would be allowed Eastern Europe and Central Europe so long as the Germans stayed away from Western Europe and any countries that came under the British Empire. This theory also holds that it was Hitler who reneged on this deal as he believed that the British would betray him at the first opportunity.

As war had broken out in 1939 and wasn't going particularly well for Britain, the prime minister at the time was removed and replaced by Winston Churchill. The previous incumbent, Neville Chamberlain, had attempted to appease the Nazis before war broke out. This had given him something of a negative reputation both with the British public and within Parliament. Churchill had been warning of the Nazi threat for over five years before the war actually broke out. His ascension to the post meant that Britain finally had a Nazi-hating Prime Minister.

Churchill became Prime Minister on the 10th of May 1940. By June, Bill had been sent to America. Bill had been informed that while he was there, he was to run the British Security Coordination. This would be a British-led intelligence agency that the Americans would use to help start up their own intelligence agency.

Bill started by getting in touch with an old American friend he had made during the First World War, Gene Tunney. As was typical of how Bill operated, he sent Gene a private letter. In the letter, he asked if Gene could facilitate a meeting with the head of the FBI, J Edgar Hoover. He told Gene that this meeting had to be secret – no one could know about it, not even the ambassador to the United States from England. Bill knew the importance of maintaining secrecy when undertaking intelligence. That was why he got in touch with someone who had friends in high places, but also someone whom he could trust.

Tunney never revealed what reason Bill had given him for the meeting remaining a secret. Whether Bill hadn't given him one or he just refused to break the trust that his friend had placed in him, we will never know, but Gene Tunney always kept a tight seal on the information.

When Bill and Hoover first met, it was a slightly cagey affair, but it did offer some measure of success. Hoover informed Bill that if they started to work together, it would break the rules about the American neutrality during the war. He told Bill that unless there was a direct order from the White House, he was unwilling to go against this rule. He also said that no other government offices should be aware of the communication between Hoover and Stephenson. This was something that Bill was more than happy to agree to – he was aware that the more people who know about something, the bigger chance there is of it being leaked. Bill informed Hoover of the suspicion that the US ambassador to England, who was notably of the opinion that the Germans were likely to win the war and that America should not get involved, had given the Germans the correspondence between Churchill and Roosevelt. Both men agreed to the terms that they laid out, and Bill started to work on getting approval from the White House.

Bill went about this by getting in touch with a lawyer friend of his who he knew had connections within the White House. Ernest Cuneo was a lawyer who worked for the Mayor of New York. Through this position, he had managed to work his way up to working with the DNC. This had given him some connections to President Roosevelt. It was this that made Bill choose him as the right person to approach. During the spring of 1940, Cuneo met with Roosevelt, who passed on the message that he wanted there to be a close link between the FBI and the British Intelligence Services. Hoover was satisfied with this, and Bill returned to England to find out the best way for him to continue his work.

Once he returned to England, things became slightly complicated for Bill. Churchill was adamant that Bill should accept the position of Passport Control Officer in New York.

This was a cover position that many Secret Intelligence Service agents would take over the years. Bill was reluctant to take the position for a few reasons. Firstly, it would mean that Bill would be replacing someone in that position, someone whom the head of the SIS didn't want to replace. This would instantly put Bill into an awkward position within the SIS, and that was the last thing that he wanted. Secondly, he didn't want to have to answer to the Americans. Bill's loyalty was to England and Churchill – he didn't want that to be undermined by a cover job.

Churchill removed these fears by having a talk with Bill before he set off back to America. He told him: 'You are to be my personal representative in the United States. I will ensure that you have the full support of all the resources at my command.'

These words made Bill feel significantly more confident that he would be able to carry out the job both effectively and without interference. He shook hands with Churchill and returned to America with a renewed sense of vigour.

He returned to America and met up with President Roosevelt. Here both men spoke about the horrors that were unfolding in Nazi Germany and the surrounding countries. They both agreed that even though America was not involved in the war, it would be vital for the FBI and the SIS to work together in terms of sharing intelligence. This would allow for the British to increase their intelligence while also ensuring that the Americans were up to date with the latest movements of the war. Bill sent word back to Britain that President Roosevelt was fully on board with the FBI and SIS working together.

Bill once again flew back to Britain, this time to prepare for a full time move to New York with his wife. Bill felt that he was to be Churchill's stateside counterpart. Everything that he did would be what he felt that Churchill wanted. His dedication to the war effort could not be questioned – his willingness to undertake a suicide mission to assassinate Hitler showed that. Bill's aim while in America was twofold. Firstly, it was to expand the intelligence reach of the British Intelligence Service and, secondly, it was to attempt to coax America into joining the war.

Bill and his wife arrived in America and stayed at the Waldorf Astoria. Bill instantly went to work. He went to the British Passport Control office and realised right away that it wouldn't be suitable for him to carry out his work. The way he saw it was that his work took precedence over almost everything else, and he needed the correct environment to carry it out. He rented an apartment that was near to Central Park and set up his office space there. Despite having a great deal of experience in working in intelligence, he had never done it in an official capacity before, and he had certainly never been in charge of the whole operation. Therefore, he felt that he would need some help. He brought in an experienced intelligence officer by the name of Charles Ellis. Ellis had been in intelligence for a long time, and Bill knew that as an Australian, he would have a different set of contacts that could be useful. Bill set about increasing the numbers for his new intelligence agency. He hired Bill Ross, John Pepper, and Walter Bell. Once they had started to become accustomed to the task at hand, Bill brought in some other men whom he trusted. AJ Taylor and Thomas Drew-Brook, his old friends from Canada, and when he was a fighter pilot, were brought into the organization. At first, it took some time for Bill to find his feet. He had spent his life as a businessman – although his early beginnings in Canada would see some people describe him as a con man – and didn't have a huge amount of experience in running intelligence. He had been able to act as a spy himself, but when it came to organizing it, he didn't know where to start.

This meant that the first few months of Bill running the new agency was a case of working out what to do. Once he had settled into the job, he decided that it would be important to try to procure additional supplies for England. The First World War had left England in quite a state. Weapons were in short supply, and it meant that the army wasn't anywhere near full strength. Bill set about creating links with as many organizations that could travel with relative impunity as possible. Nurse groups, the Salvation Army, and many others all became potential targets and allies. He intended to get them to help get extra supplies for England as well as then get them across the ocean.

It wasn't an easy job, as America was reluctant to join in the war effort. They felt that involving themselves in the First World War had been a mistake and that what the Germans, and to a lesser extent the Japanese, were planning was none of their concern. This wasn't helped by the US ambassador consistently informing President Roosevelt that joining the war would be a mistake as Britain would be defeated within a month. This may have been the ambassador's Nazi tendencies coming into play, a theory that was put forward by more than one person close to him.

Regardless of the personal beliefs of the US ambassador, the American people still believed that joining in the war would be a mistake. The economic trouble that the First World War had caused America, mainly in the form of unpaid debts from European countries, had led them to believe that Europe had nothing to offer them. America had started to isolate itself, and even though Roosevelt was worried about the Nazis, he was still unsure about helping in the war as he felt it would harm America more in the long run.

Bill knew that getting supplies for England would be a tough battle for him. Therefore, he turned to a man whom he called an old friend: Bill Donovan. It was surprising to many that the two men were so well acquainted, purely because there were so many different stories about how they had first met. Perhaps fittingly for two of the most important intelligence officers of the Second World War, the truth of how they met will possibly never be known. Some believe that they first met during the First World War, and some think that they met when carrying out business deals in the 30s. Whatever the case of their first meeting, both men classed each other as friends and were more than willing to help each other out wherever they could. Bill is said to have used the telephone to contact Donovan as soon as he landed in America in June of 1940, and they met up as soon as possible afterwards. From here, Donovan helped Bill to meet with the relevant people who could help Britain when it came to the problem of their lack of destroyers and other military equipment.

Donovan helped Bill to meet with the Secretary of the Navy, Secretary of War, and Secretary of State. Bill's aim was to find out exactly how much help he could get from the Americans without them breaking their neutrality. Bill wanted the American Navy to transfer fifty of their older destroyer ships to the Royal Navy. He felt that this was the most likely way to bolster the Royal Navy without breaking any laws. Bill suggested that Donovan visit Britain to take a look at exactly what was needed. It was a trip that was presented as an appraisal of the British chances during the war, but really it was to see where the best places for American help could be applied.

Bill used his contacts both in Washington and London to plan out Donovan's trip. He avoided the embassy because of both the lack of trust he had in them as well as their inability to get Donovan into the places Bill needed him to be.

Donovan made his way to Britain and looked at the different areas that Britain needed help. When he returned to Washington, he made it clear that Britain would be able to more than hold their own in the war, but they did need some help in terms of armaments. They had lost a lot of equipment at Dunkirk, and this had left the British Army and Navy in quite a perilous situation. Part of the reason that Bill was trusted so much by the Americans was that he was Canadian. This meant that they saw him as an independent rather than a British man who was just trying to get something for nothing. They felt that his worry about the Nazis wasn't just based on their taking over Britain – it was based on more of a long-term view that encompassed the safety and security of Canada, and as such also included the safety and security of the United States.

Donovan made his way to England in July of 1940. He didn't stop by in the American embassy. Even though they had been bypassed in the organization of the trip, it would have been expected of him to stop in at some point. Bill and Donovan both felt that it was better to avoid the embassy entirely as the ambassador had declined an official visit for Donovan earlier in the year and because they felt that he was untrustworthy. By avoiding the embassy, it also meant that Donovan could avoid any potentially awkward questions about the nature of his visit.

Donovan spent a total of two weeks in England. During this time, he met with a host of prestigious individuals flaunting varying amounts of wealth and prominence. He was using the trip not just to see what Britain had the greatest need for in terms of additional supplies, but also to build up his own base of contacts. As well as networking with influential individuals, he was also learning from the different departments within the British war machine. Included in this was the Secret Intelligence Service. This meant that when he returned to America, he would be in a better place to start up an American operation of a similar nature. Despite the current lack of desire from the higher-ups in Washington to get directly involved in the war, Donovan still knew that it was vital to have as much intelligence as possible about any conflict that was happening in the world. All it took was one incident for the Americans to be drawn into it, and he didn't want them to be going in blind.

In early August of 1940, Donovan returned to America. He had decided on four main points he needed to deliver to Roosevelt when he returned. Firstly, that Britain didn't know when they were defeated. They could continue fighting even when all hope was lost. Secondly, that even though they had great determination, it was likely that they would lose unless they got the supplies that they needed. Thirdly, the supplies needed to be taken straight to the front lines, not delivered elsewhere and then distributed. Finally, the Americans needed to both challenge fifth column activity and embark on their own course of it.

Fifth column activity was blamed heavily for the capitulation of France early on in the conflict. The Germans had people working undercover in France to stoke up pro-Nazi feeling, and this led to the country as a whole being in a much weaker state. Donovan was worried that this was being undertaken in America. The public was fervently against joining the war at this point. While President Roosevelt and his advisors were all generally in line with this way of thinking, Donovan believed that the public felt like this because subtle fifth column activists had been stoking anti-war feeling within the country. He decided that the government needed to engage in their own fifth column activities, although they wouldn't be as subtle about it as the Germans.

Donovan attacked this head on when he returned. Instead of setting up small groups around the country who would try to increase support for joining the war, he wrote articles in newspapers that warned of what the Nazis had been doing. He also addressed the country on television, warning them of

German fifth columnists. He felt that this would be more effective as it would warn people that the Nazis were among them and help to turn support towards joining the war, especially if the American people felt like they could potentially be a target.

Once he had done this, he turned his hand to ensuring that the British could get the destroyers that they needed. Donovan, along with the Secretary of the Navy, pressured the president at every opportunity. They pushed him to give the destroyers even though there was staunch opposition, especially from the president's advisors. Despite the opposition, it didn't take too long for Donovan to convince Roosevelt that sending the destroyers to the British was the right move.

On the 22nd of August, Bill Stephenson let the powers that be in London know that the deal for the destroyers had been completed. By the start of September, the deal had been announced to the wider cabinet. A great number of people within the cabinet at the time credited the job to the hard work of Bill. He wasn't so quick to accept complete credit for it though. Bill was always adamant that if it hadn't been for the help of Bill Donovan, the deal would never have got over the line. He knew that he had been the one who had brought Donovan into play and that it was his own contacts that made the initial movements in the deal possible, but he also knew that without Donovan he would have been fighting a losing battle.

It wasn't just the destroyers that Bill managed to procure for the British, either. He also managed to gain a flying fortress and over one million rifles, which were given to the home guard. The British Security Coordination, as Bill's operation was known, also organised and deployed security patrols that ran 24 hours a day, seven days a week across all major transport hubs where supplies were being run. In a short time, they had managed to move from not really knowing what to do to getting a huge amount of supplies for the British war effort and running a large scale security operation. It was a highly impressive rise from almost humble beginnings. The BSC also moved into other areas. They started getting information about Japanese industry and creating fake documents to throw the Germans off the scent.

Bill knew that it was getting too much for them in their small office in his rented apartment. They needed to expand, not just their premises but their personnel as well. He decided to move to Rockefeller Centre. It was a high-profile building, but it meant that they would have a significant amount of extra space as well as being more attractive to potential employees. AJ Taylor and Thomas Drew-Brook were put in charge of finding new members of their team. They went to Canada for new recruits. They brought in a professor at the University of Toronto, a journalist, and an investment dealer.

They didn't just bring in people in important jobs, though – they brought in regular people, too.

To bring in more workers, a newspaper advert was placed in Canadian newspapers. It didn't mention that intelligence work would be carried out – obviously, the Germans would have people looking out for that kind of thing – but it did mention that it involved secretarial work for the British government based in New York. Through these newspaper adverts, over 800 employees were brought on board at the BSC. All records of the BSC were destroyed at the end of the war, so no names are available for the workers who carried out secretarial work, but they still carried out a highly important job during the war. Bill had been known as The Quiet Canadian; what is surprising is just how many Canadians also kept quiet about their contribution to the war effort. Perhaps it was that they had been kept in the dark by being given roles that could easily have been seen as just admin work. Or perhaps it was just the attitudes that members of intelligence had to talk about work. Either way, the Canadian impact on the war cannot be downplayed.

The next step for the BSC was to combat the anti-war feeling within America. There were a great deal of American isolationist movements within America at the time of the war. A lot of this came from bad feeling after the unpaid debts of the First World War, but there was also a more sinister reason.

There was a lot of fifth column activity within America during the Second World War. There were a lot of German-Americans who wanted America to stay out of the war. While they weren't great in number, they did have money to devote to their cause. A lot of this was funded and fuelled by Nazi propaganda, but there was an anti-war feeling that emanated purely from the American side of things. Bill and the BSC instantly started to put their own fifth column plans into action.

The first step that Bill and the BSC took was to start getting their employees to join up with the different movements. From there, they could keep track of the members and what their plans were. The second step that Bill took was to use his contacts within the media to start to attack the anti-war fifth columnists. Journalists at *The New York Post, The New York Times, The Baltimore Sun,* and *The New York Herald Tribune* were all brought on board by Bill. They wrote sympathetic articles towards the British and their war efforts in an attempt to gently soften the attitude of most Americans towards joining the war. At the time of Bill's move to New York, nine out of 10 Americans were against the war, and there was even an American Nazi party who were hell-bent on America joining the war on the same side as the Germans!

Once Bill had the newspapers on board, he started to move towards other areas of the media. The BSC took control of a popular New York radio station, WRUL. From here, the BSC started to pump out propaganda of their own. They made sure that the listeners were slowly indoctrinated to believe that joining the war was the only sensible choice. There were a range of news bulletins offering a pro-British slant on all news based around the war and was completely run by Bill's people at the BSC.

The BSC also made attempts to shift the views of anti-British newspapers, as well. When this wasn't effective, then a move to a much more aggressive tactic was made. Bill approached the British government asking for a huge amount of money to buy the debts that the Hearst newspaper chain had to a Canadian company. From there, they would be able to control the chain, either by using their ownership of their debts to get them to change their stance or by shutting them down completely. Unfortunately for Bill, the government refused to sanction such a large amount of money, and it was one of the few times that his requests were turned down.

Another aggressive tactic that the BSC employed was to target and harass specific isolationist groups. For example, when a staunch supporter of isolationism, who also happened to be a senator, spoke at a rally, Bill's people handed out leaflets attacking him on a personal level and claiming that he was a Nazi supporter. Another speech by a representative named Hamilton Fish had a card delivered to him saying 'Der

Fuhrer thanks you for your loyalty'. After the war ended, it was discovered that Fish had indeed had financial support from German sources, but whether this had any ties to his being a Nazi supporter is unknown. It was something he always denied, and he even attempted to sue someone who claimed that he was, although the case was thrown out and he never settled.

Bill knew that getting the Americans to join the war was the most critical aspect of his mission. Therefore, the BSC began to devote more time and effort in breaking down the groups who spearheaded the American isolationist movement. Through anti-isolationist groups, Bill started to find people who would be willing to work as double agents for his cause. The first man that he managed to make contact with was Donald Downes. He had joined a group called the Free World Association. This was a group that was mainly made up of people who had escaped from Nazi-occupied countries. As such, they were more than aware of the horrors that were being committed by them.

Downes was asked to join the America First group. The America First group were the hard-line American isolationists. Bill and the BSC had suspicions that they were much more sinister than that, though. The BSC thought that America First was actually a front for the Nazi party. Downes infiltrated the group and helped the BSC to find their largest slice of intelligence so far. Downes managed to find out information about a wide range of pro-Nazi people who had infiltrated places such as the German embassy, the Italian Embassy, and even General Motors. He cast his net wide and provided information for the BSC about Nazi activity in New York, Boston, San Francisco, Cleveland, Chicago, and Washington. A lot of the information that Downes provided was of great use to the BSC, but it didn't serve the original purpose that Bill had intended it to.

The information had originally been collected to help turn the tide of American public opinion about joining in the war. That all changed in December of 1941 when the Japanese attacked Pearl Harbor, forcing the Americans to join the war as their forces had been stationed there. While the information still meant that Bill had a large portfolio of information on Nazi activity in America, this meant that Bill's job had changed slightly. He was no longer in America to persuade America to join the war – he was there to coordinate all of the intelligence on the Allies' enemies.

Chapter 5: An Intelligence Trailblazer

Even before the Americans had joined the war officially, it was well known within official circles that President Roosevelt was not satisfied with the intelligence services that America had to offer. Apart from the FBI, there was no agency that gathered information for them. This meant that they were slightly behind other countries when it came to knowing what was going in the world. Part of the problem they had was that in addition to each branch of the military having limited resources in regards to intelligence, they also saw each other as competition and possibly did not trust each other either.

As the possibility of Britain falling to the Nazis became more likely, especially after Dunkirk, the Americans realised that it was necessary to begin setting up intelligence of their own. They couldn't keep relying on Britain to supply their intelligence for them. Therefore, Roosevelt set up the

Coordinator of Information, the COI, in the middle of 1941. For Roosevelt, there was only one choice: Bill Donovan.

Donovan was the obvious choice for the President. He had a range of experience as a lawyer and public servant. He had also been a soldier and a highly decorated one at that. This meant that he was well versed in making sure of the facts and had a great deal of respect from most people within Washington. From Roosevelt's side, it also made sense to use Donovan because he was a Republican. As Roosevelt was a Democrat, the fewer powerful Republicans there were against him, the better.

Despite all of this, Donovan found it very difficult to make the switch to working in intelligence. Although he had helped to facilitate Bill Stephenson when it came to getting additional supplies for Britain, he had no real experience of working intelligence. Fortunately, Bill Donovan and Bill Stephenson had remained close. Stephenson knew that Donovan would require his help, and he felt as though he owed him after he had helped him early on in his mission to America. He provided a wide range of background information when it came to setting up intelligence and security channels. In addition to this, Bill used his own experienced intelligence officers to train the COI recruits. They were taken to Canada, and Thomas Drew-Brook organised and carried out a lot of the training. It was the first spy school in America, and although Bill Donovan gained a large amount of credit for the success of the COI during the Second World War, the influence and help of Bill Stephenson cannot be underestimated.

Because of this training school, as well as the other help that Bill provided, the Americans actually had managed to set up a functioning intelligence agency in half the time it would usually take. Bill had repaid a favour to his friend, but it wasn't a completely selfless act. He knew that if the Americans were collecting their own intelligence, then their alliance would see their intelligence being shared. It meant that even though it cost the resources of the BSC to train the American agents, in the long run, it would allow them to spend their resources elsewhere as the Americans would be gathering intelligence that they would have access to.

Bill had been expanding his influence across a range of areas during the time he had been head of the BSC. He even managed to arrange Nöel Coward a tour of South Africa, such was the influence that Bill Stephenson wielded at this point. Bill also ensured that the training camp for COI agents became a communications centre that linked all of the most essential parts of the Allied war effort. The BSC at this point was funded by the British, but it was a truly worldwide operation. Bill also maintained a high level of cooperation with the COI, willingly sharing information that his agency had collected in return for information that the COI had collected. It ensured that both agencies had a wide range of intelligence, but the cost to one single agency was limited. Bill also took Donovan to Britain with him to help him establish a contact in both the British Navy and British Army. Bill was making sure that his friends had access to almost as much as he did to make sure that they were as useful to him as possible.

By October of 1941, President Roosevelt had informed Churchill of the creation of the COI and that Bill Donovan had been given the job. He also informed him that he intended to set up a London-based office. Regardless of what Churchill's own feelings were about an American intelligence office being based in London, it wasn't something that he could turn down due to his own intelligence agency having an American-based office for such a long period. Another reason that he wouldn't be averse to it was that Churchill knew that the COI officers had been trained by British agents. Roosevelt informed him that because of this help, the COI would be charged with directly helping the British war effort.

Donovan once again went to Bill Stephenson for help. Although the British government had been aware that he had helped Donovan set up the COI, Bill kept his involvement in the next stage secret. He helped Donovan with creating his headquarters and used one of his best men, Ian Fleming – who went on to worldwide fame as the creator of James Bond – to help create some notes for the COI.

Bill also helped to fill in any gaps that the COI had with his own men. This went on from when the COI was first set up until well into 1942, so after the Pearl Harbor attack and America officially joining the war. This aspect of Bill's help was not well known within Britain and wasn't something that they would have been entirely pleased about. It wasn't that the Americans weren't trusted by the British, it was more because they were inexperienced in intelligence matters and the British didn't want information to be accidentally leaked.

Bill Stephenson disagreed with this stance. He recognised that an American intelligence agency that was performing well was an asset to Britain. He also knew that as his own officers had trained the agents for the COI, they were of the highest standard. Although it was kept secret, by the middle of 1942 British agencies had got used to the Americans being involved, even on the periphery of their operations, with intelligence exchanges. Bill knew that the Americans could be an incredible ally to Britain, but he also knew that they needed help to become that ally. That was why he dedicated so much time and so many resources to making sure that they were fully prepared.

Bill Stephenson and Bill Donovan both made many trips back and forth to the different intelligence bases that the BSC had set up during the war. One such trip to Bermuda was for Donovan to check out the operation that was in place to filter mail. It was here that all censoring was carried out before it was relayed to its eventual destination. All pieces of mail were checked for ciphers, secret ink, and other potential methods of sending information secretly. It was here that a microdot was first discovered, and from then on the checking process was refined to ensure that no microdots got through. Bill was immensely proud of his work in Bermuda, and he felt that it was almost perfect.

Bill Donovan had met with Churchill, through Bill Stephenson, as early as December 1940. It was here that Churchill informed Donovan of the German plan to attack the Soviet Union. From here, Donovan carried on to Yugoslavia and had documents stolen from him by Nazi agents that had been following him. What the Nazi agents didn't know was that this had been planned and the papers that were stolen were phony. This led to a change of plan from the Nazis because of the fake information that Bill Donovan had passed on. It was this kind of operation that Bill Stephenson felt vindicated his decision to help the Americans. Because at that point in the war they were officially involved, he knew that there wouldn't be any suspicion about Donovan carrying fake papers.

By 1942, Bill had moved on the activities of the BSC into not just intelligence but also helping to arm resistance factions around Europe. He even helped with moving Niels Bohr, a highly regarded nuclear physicist, away from the Nazis and to the Manhattan Project, which notably created the first atomic bombs, which were used during the war.

    Bill was also meeting with Churchill almost every time that he returned to Britain during the war. There are at least 30 documented visits, but as Bill regularly travelled under fake names and a lot of documents were destroyed after the war, there could have been many more visits than were recorded. Churchill felt that America joining the war was the only way that Britain could possibly win. He knew that the Germans were significantly better equipped than they were – after all, he had been warning the British Government for more than five years before war broke out that the Germans were rearming, but no one had listened to him. Churchill also knew that Bill Stephenson was highly important in gaining American support. Not only was he coordinating one of the most effective and complicated intelligence operations that the world had ever seen, but he also had a great deal of support from President Roosevelt. In fact, it is said that Bill was the only man that both Churchill and Roosevelt both trusted implicitly. His ability to get the ear of both men meant that in terms of British and American collaboration, he was the glue that held it all together.

    Perhaps all the more impressive is that he managed to continue with his business interests during this time. His personal secretary was based in England throughout the war, and it was her responsibility to maintain Bill's businesses while also keeping him completely up to date with how they were going. She worked full time at a time when very few women did so. She also did an excellent job, which was shown in the way that Bill kept her on as his full-time employee at least for the duration of the war.

One of the most intelligent shifts he made as war broke out was to change a lot of his businesses to create items and equipment that could help with the war effort. His cement businesses were used to help to build fortifications, and his aircraft businesses had a much more obvious wartime occupation. Even the film studios that he had invested in were used to build decoy weapons to help fool the enemy without using a lot of resources.

While Bill spent a great deal of the war in New York, one area that was inadvertently helping him were the activities of his friends. They were spending their time building up a large base of contacts with people high up within the American political and military hierarchy. While some of his friends were doing this without really realising that they were helping Bill, some of them, such as AJ Taylor, were building up contacts deliberately as part of their work for the BSC. Bill's list of contacts was growing by the day.

The mail-checking facility at Bermuda was actually made to be even more stringent in October of 1941, just before the Americans joined the war. This occurred by accident as a man working in the New York centre realised that letters being sent to people on the security blacklist in London were getting their mail delivered unopened. There had obviously been a crossing of wires at some point, and once this had been discovered, the practice was changed to ensure that all mail was checked, no matter what. This led to Bill creating the BSC mail intercept service, which made the whole process both highly detailed and incredibly fast. By November of 1941, it was obvious that the Japanese and Americans would be unable to negotiate their way through their disagreements. It was at this point that Donovan asked Bill for any information from mail that passed through Hong Kong and Singapore. Bill was more than happy to help the Americans and made sure that the relevant information was passed on to his team.

The interception of mail took up quite a large amount of time and resources, but Bill knew that in terms of value, it paid them back tenfold. That was why he dedicated such a large amount of time to making sure that the system worked at its absolute best. They didn't just check the mail; they used skills from various chemists and language experts to make sure that no matter what was coming through at their ports they would be able to spot any secret messages.

By the early parts of 1941, Bill had begun to make contact with the British embassy based in Washington. Lord Halifax wasn't a man that Bill felt fondly about, but he was aware that he needed to remain on good terms for the good of the war effort. Through the British embassy, Bill was able to gain access to other ambassadors that he felt were untrustworthy. The French embassy had an employee who, through intelligence, Bill had found to be suspicious. Bill had his agents tap his telephone and bug his meeting room. He didn't care for the legalities of what he was doing – he believed the man to be a Nazi sympathiser, and for that reason, he was going to use him to gain as much information as possible.

Bill also used an agent who had the codename 'Cynthia'. She started a romantic liaison with the press attaché for the French embassy. From here, she was able to gain access to a wide range of papers and even French Navy ciphers. She began memorising conversations when at dinner and recording whom the ambassador had met up with. Once she had collated enough information, she presented it to Bill. Bill prepared a report and took it directly to President Roosevelt. In what can only be described as a sneaky trick, he also leaked some of the report to the *New York Herald Times*. This ensured that the general public was aware that parts of their country had been penetrated by the Nazis. This was carried out in September of 1941 before America had officially joined the war, but it was an incredibly effective way to help turn the tide of public opinion. Although it wasn't needed in the end due to the Pearl Harbor attacks, it was still important to get the American public onside with helping the British rather than just looking out for their own interests.

The BSC didn't just hit the French embassy though. They also penetrated the Mexican, Japanese, and Colombian embassies. This ensured that they had a wide range of information from both potential Nazi sympathisers and people already acting in the interests of the Nazis. The BSC even used the janitor at the Spanish embassy to find out as much information as possible from there. Bill's team had no limit to what they were prepared to do to find out the information that they required.

Bill's work didn't just encompass finding out intelligence, though. During the early 1940s, he spent a lot of his time both protecting and learning from scientists. Chaim Weizmann, Albert Einstein, and Henry Tizard were all under Bill's protection at one time or another. He used this time to learn as much as he could from these men as well as protect them. Tizard, in particular, was of great use to the Americans as he shared a number of secrets that the British had developed in order to help them with their own war effort. Both the radar and jet engine made their way across the Atlantic courtesy of Tizard.

The BSC continued to grow. By 1942, it had more files than their clerks could handle. They had to quickly employ several filing clerks, and they even brought in a filing expert from Canada to help them in the short term. The BSC was building up a database of everyone of importance as well as all links that they had to other people. It was an incredible amount of work in the pre-computer age. The BSC collected information on every aspect of any person of interest's life – from close friends to family members, to sports clubs they were members of. Anything was added because Bill knew that even the slightest of details could become massively important in the future. The intelligence that they had collected also tried to work out who the BSC would be most likely to have a chance of blackmailing. Anyone who had debts or family members in trouble would be susceptible to blackmail, and the BSC knew that this would be one of the most effective ways to get intelligence. Not just intelligence, reliable and valuable intelligence. This huge amount of information was vital to Bill's work, and keeping it organised had started to become a problem, Although at first, the Americans had been happy for Bill to work within their country, the rapid growth of the BSC had led to some rumblings within the bureaucratic network.

J Edgar Hoover was obviously aware that Bill was working within America, and he had some idea of what the BSC was doing although of course he wasn't aware of the extent of the BSC operations. The first signs of there being a problem within America with what the BSC was doing was in February 1941. An FBI agent reported that Bill Stephenson wasn't known to anyone within the FBI or any other agencies.

He also reported that the police weren't aware of him and that he was keeping the location of his offices a secret. This coincided with Bill's job description being changed from Passport Control Officer to Director of Security Coordination in the US. While both of these job descriptions explained very little, as they were cover positions, what Bill was actually doing was working as the main representative for MI6 within the entire Western Hemisphere. At this point, very few people within America – Bill Donovan and President Roosevelt are thought to be two of them – were actually aware of what he was doing. This meant that people further down the political and bureaucratic ladder were about to start causing trouble for Bill and the BSC.

By March of 1941, the Assistant Secretary of State had sent a letter expressing his concern for the size of the BSC. He was aware that Bill was the head of the BSC and was worried about the number of places in America that had BSC offices. He claimed that the BSC was violating American laws and that it would cause a huge amount of friction when it came to explaining why the BSC had been allowed to carry out its mission. He felt that if an investigation was carried out, it could spell bad news for a large number of people within Washington. Although the Assistant Secretary of State pointed out this information in March of 1941, it took almost twelve months for the situation to really become a problem.

In February of 1942, The Assistant Secretary of State

lobbied President Roosevelt to implement the McKellar Bill. This meant that all foreign agents would either be expelled from the country or made to register, and their activities would be closely monitored by the American government. He wrote to the President claiming that the Director of Security Coordination title that Bill had been given was nothing but a name. In reality, he was the head of British espionage – something that President Roosevelt was fully aware of, but the Assistant Secretary of State was not.

Once the McKellar Bill had been put in place, it didn't take long for Bill to start work on getting it thrown out. First, he approached the British embassy. They informed Bill that they didn't have the sufficient power to stop it from being put into place. Bill decided to go to his old friend Bill Donovan. He knew that Bill Donovan would do what he could to get it vetoed. Donovan sent a memo to the President asking for the bill to be vetoed. As well as Donovan, Bill got in touch with another contact of his who was close to the President: his speechwriter, Robert Sherwood. He told the President that the bill was a leftover of isolationism and would do nothing to help America in the long run. All of Bill's lobbying worked as the bill was vetoed on the 9th of February, 1942. Despite the bill being vetoed, Bill was still worried. He felt that a lot of anti-British attitudes were creeping into not just the American public but the higher-ups within Washington. He knew that the President didn't currently have this type of feeling, but he was worried that it could creep in if it were allowed to keep running unchecked.

On the day that the President vetoed the bill, Bill instantly gathered his staff and asked for ideas on how they could improve the relationship between America and Britain. He needed the Americans to feel that a British intelligence agency on their shores was useful.

Things got worse for Bill and the BSC as February continued moving forward. One of his agents was expelled from the country for his actions. There are two versions of this story, with no one knowing the actual truth. The first version is that the agent was tailing the Assistant Secretary of State in order to gather information on him that the BSC could use to their advantage. The FBI caught him in the act of doing this, and because of that, he was expelled from the country. The other version is that the agent was doing no such thing, and the FBI had set him up to make themselves look good. Whatever the truth was, it wasn't a situation that Bill needed at that moment. He was already under intense scrutiny, and this just turned up the heat a couple of notches.

At the end of February, a meeting took place between some important people that would cause Bill and the BSC another headache. The Attorney General, J Edgar Hoover, the Assistant Secretary of State, Admiral Wilkinson, and General Raymond Lee all met up to discuss the BSC. The general consensus between the men was that the BSC had been set up at least before the Americans had joined in with the war and possibly before the war had even started. They believed the President was aware of its existence and that he had agreed to it being created. What they didn't know was if the President was aware of what it had grown into. They were also concerned about the large volume of coded messages that was being sent through the FBI radio each month. They decided that something needed to be done about the BSC, and as they knew that Bill Stephenson had friends in high places, it would possibly need to be done without the President knowing about it.

In early March, the Attorney General, the Assistant Secretary of State, and J Edgar Hoover met with the British ambassador and a British minister. Almost instantly, the two British representatives were ambushed with talk about how the duties of the BSC needed to be toned down. The Americans wanted the BSC to work as a liaison operation only and wanted the number of agents that they had employed drastically reduced. In response to this, the British ambassador replied that the BSC didn't do anything without the explicit permission of the FBI and that there was an exchange of intelligence going on between the two agencies. Hoover instantly countered that this was not the case. He informed the ambassador that he frequently only found out what the BSC was doing after the fact, and often only because he had been informed by someone else. He also said that he felt like Bill Stephenson was lying to the FBI about the information that he was passing over. They told the ambassador that they had no problem with Bill on a personal level but felt that he wasn't the right man to be the head of their intelligence operation. Hoover informed the ambassador that there wasn't a close relationship between the FBI and the BSC and while Bill was in charge, or at least while he was running it in the manner that he was, it was highly unlikely that there ever would be. The ambassador took all of this on board but was shocked at the revelations.

Just five days later, the Assistant Secretary of State noted that he was highly distressed by the volume of messages that the BSC was sending back to British Intelligence in London each week. Over 300 messages were being sent each week, and as they all used British ciphers, the Americans had no idea what they said. The Assistant Secretary of State was informed that they were private messages between Roosevelt and Churchill, but he didn't believe that claim. He felt that the BSC was lying to him. That meant that either the agents were lying to him off their own backs, or Bill Stephenson had told them to lie to him. Either one was unacceptable to him. It was at this point that he realised that Bill must have people on the inside of Donovan's operation, perhaps through transferring them onto his payroll. The Assistant Secretary of State didn't realise that Bill's team had trained the vast majority of Donovan's men, and it was this reason that he was able to use resources that they had available so easily.

The problems from the Assistant Secretary of State died down slightly at this point, but that wasn't the end of people attempting to remove Bill from his position. In 1943, there were rumours that a man named GC Denham was going to take over from Bill as the head of the BSC. This could have been a case of crossed wires as Denham ended up taking over the position as head of MI5 in the US. These challenges to his position meant that Bill made sure that both he and his officers were more careful. He wanted to make sure that the relationship between the US and Britain, at least in terms of their intelligence agencies, was a cordial one. He knew that the sharing of information would make his job easier, and he didn't want to lose that.

Because Bill was in charge of the whole of the Western hemisphere, it wasn't just the United States of America that he had to worry about. He also had to keep an eye on South America. He knew that it was vulnerable to fifth column activity from Nazis – they saw it as an easy place to infiltrate and were hoping to set up a base of operations that would allow for a much easier passage into the USA if the time ever arose.

The first real rumblings about this issue first came about

in May of 1941. The American ambassador to Columbia was talking to a journalist whom he knew. He told the journalist that he was worried about the lack of intelligence in South America. He felt that the region had been left to rot and as a result, the wrong people had got hold of the country and moulded it in whatever fashion they pleased. The journalist told the ambassador about the work Bill Donovan had been doing with Bill Stephenson. He told him about how Nazi fifth column activity worked and that Donovan had been taking trips to Europe with Bill Stephenson to find out how it worked and how to combat it. The ambassador felt that this was exactly what was happening in South America, so the journalist arranged a meeting with Donovan for him.

Once the ambassador met with Donovan, his worst fears were confirmed. Everything that Donovan laid out to him, from propaganda to sabotage, was taking place in Columbia, for definite, and most likely across the rest of South America. The ambassador was incredibly worried, so Donovan asked him if he would like him to arrange a meeting with the head of British intelligence. While most people in the American system wouldn't have deferred to someone like Bill in this manner, Donovan knew exactly how useful Bill was and what his job really was. The ambassador was extremely thankful and confirmed that he would be grateful if a meeting could be arranged.

The meeting with Bill was far more productive than the

ambassador ever could have hoped. Bill met him and informed him almost instantly that he intended to keep a closer eye on South America. He told him that he was going to reorganise the intelligence operation in South America and that the ambassador would be having an agent named Stagg sent to him. Stagg's cover was that he was a playboy. He was to live the high life in Columbia in order not to bring suspicion about his real occupation. However, he would be reporting to the ambassador any relevant information.

Stagg and his wife made the trip over to Columbia from nearby Ecuador. Once he arrived, he instantly fell into the playboy act. Stagg started throwing lavish parties, going out all night dancing, and spending his days playing tennis. He played the part of a playboy to a tee. Despite this, Stagg was very competent when it came to his work. Even when he was out partying, he was still working. He spent his evenings at parties that contained the right people to find out all of the information he needed to help the ambassador. Whenever Stagg appeared at the embassy, he was given complete priority. People couldn't understand why – they thought it was a case of Stagg having friends in high places, but they still couldn't work out why the ambassador would cancel meetings to meet with Stagg. It never raised suspicion that Stagg was anything more than a good friend of the ambassador, though, which meant that Stagg's work could go ahead unhindered.

Part of what helped his work was that the American ambassador in Columbia wanted it. It wasn't like the Americans, who felt threatened by Bill and the BSC's work.

One such example of the ambassador putting his trust in Stagg was when there was a large meeting at the German Legation. He informed Stagg, and within minutes, he was walking past the legation with his wife and another agent. The other agent was able to memorise every single license plate of the cars at the meeting. Stagg had chosen a man with an eidetic memory specifically for the job, so he was able to remember each plate with complete clarity. When they returned to the embassy, he wrote down all of the plates for the ambassador, which allowed for a trace to be run on all of the plates, and they were able to find out that everyone at the meeting had ties to the Nazi party.

One such example where Stagg used his position to help the Allied war effort while also taking advantage of the American ambassador in Columbia was with the situation in Bolivia. The BSC had heard rumours of a coup being planned in Bolivia by a German minister by the name of Belmonte. When they found this out, they jumped into action. There are two stories as to what happened next. The first story is that they forged a letter saying that they had intercepted a transcript of the letter about Belmonte planning his coup. The second story is that they actually did intercept the letter in Buenos Aires. Stagg told the ambassador that the letter had been intercepted and that they wanted the Americans to steal the diplomatic pouch in order to get hold of the original. The ambassador asked by the American State Department refused to engage with such a plan. After this, Bill heard from J Edgar Hoover that Belmonte was planning a coup, so the letter was read over the radio verbatim. This led to the Bolivian government breaking off diplomatic relations with Germany and expelling Belmonte from the country. This was an excellent development for the allies as it meant that the Germans wouldn't have access to as much wolfram, which they used in arms manufacture.

The BSC continued to work throughout the war, and they started to keep track of all of the money flowing in and out of South America. Bill's office was used as a liaison point for intelligence services in both the USA and Canada. After suffering some pushback earlier in the 1940s, the Americans had finally realised that his work was of great use and he was an important part of making their own intelligence function efficiently. Bill was in charge of a lot of different areas of intelligence. He oversaw the building of the Camp X training centre, which had been used to train both the BSC agents and Donovan's people. He monitored the flow of money, people, mail, and supplies both in and out of Europe. He was in charge of intelligence for the whole of the Western Hemisphere. He managed to do all of this in the age before computers. This meant that messages were much more difficult to send quickly and securely. It meant that tracing people and cross-referencing things was a much more arduous task. While he wouldn't have been doing those jobs personally as the BSC had clerks for such a task, it did mean that he wasn't able to get the information he needed to do his job as quickly as he would have in the modern world.

As the war drew to a close, Bill was honoured by the British. They knighted him in 1944, although it wasn't publicly announced until the 1st of January, 1945. In a surprising twist, J Edgar Hoover wrote a letter to Bill congratulating him on the honour and telling him that he deserved it for his immense contribution to the war effort. It appeared that by the end of the war, the FBI head had realised just how much of a positive contribution Bill had made to the Allied war effort. Perhaps Donovan had told him just how much Bill had done for the Americans; whatever the reason, Bill was almost as pleased to receive the letter from Hoover as he was to receive the knighthood.

Not long after he was knighted, Bill Donovan decided that the Americans should also honour Bill. After all, he had been a huge part of the success of the COI and the Office of Strategic Services. Without Bill, neither of them would have been fit for purpose in time to have had any positive impact on the war. Donovan was one of the few people who were completely aware of this, and he felt that the efforts Bill had put in were worthy of recognition. The Americans didn't agree at the time – they felt that before medals were awarded, the war should be won. They were true to their word. In 1946, Bill was awarded the American Distinguished Service Medal. Bill was the first foreigner to be awarded this medal, which was at the time of the award the highest civilian award possible. What tarnished the award slightly was that the British Foreign Office hadn't given their formal approval for Bill to be awarded the medal. President Roosevelt and Bill Donovan went ahead with awarding the medal to Bill anyway. They knew just how much he had given to the American war effort. It took Bill's homeland slightly longer to recognise his achievements. But in 1979, he was made a Companion of the Order of Canada.

While Bill wasn't directly involved in the creation of the CIA, it is important to recognise just how much his influence was present when it was set up. After the war, both the COI and OSS were disbanded. This led to the agents from both organisations being absorbed by the military and Navy. It didn't last long, and the CIA was formed not long after, using people that the BSC had trained and using a wide range of the methods that Bill had introduced to American soil. Donovan was shocked that the British government wasn't more enthusiastic about Bill receiving the medal as it demonstrated to the world that their intelligence was the best in the world.

Once the war was over, Bill had two more things to take care of. First, he collated every single file that the BSC had acquired during the war and took it all to Camp X. Here, he had several agents and clerks summarise it down into a single book. This book only had 20 copies printed and one of the writers, Tom Hill, was given 10 of those copies. After a year, he didn't want the responsibility of looking after them anymore – they were classified as top secret and, in fact, still are to this day – so he asked Bill if he wanted them. Bill said he didn't, so Tom took them to his wife's family farm and burned them. The book was so in depth and had methods so far ahead of its time that it is referred to as 'The Bible' by MI6 and still used to this day.

His final mission took place in September of 1945. Bill was supposed to meet with the Canadian Prime Minister, Mackenzie King, but King was taken ill and was unable to meet with Bill. Instead, he met with Norman Robertson, who was the Under Secretary of State in External Affairs at the time. It was here that he heard some information that piqued his interest. A cipher clerk at the Soviet Embassy by the name of Igor Gouzenko had been working for the Soviet Military Intelligence. During his time working in intelligence, he had realised that what his government was doing was wrong. He had seen how caring the people of Canada were – they had been sending money and supplies to the Soviets to help the Soviet citizens. What really upset him was that the Soviet government had been creating an espionage network within Canada to take advantage as soon as any weakness was shown. Gouzenko felt that this was against the interests of the Soviet citizens as the Canadians had been helping them, and for their government to then attempt to stab Canada in the back at the first opportunity was an inherently wrong thing to do.

Gouzenko made the mistake of committing a security breach, and he and his pregnant wife were ordered to return home to the Soviet Union. This wasn't something Gouzenko wanted to do as he knew what would be awaiting them there. Instead of returning home, they decided to remain in Canada. What really piqued Bill's interest was that Gouzenko and his wife had not been offered any form of protection. In fact, the Canadian Prime Minister felt that suicide would be the only way out for Gouzenko. Bill felt that this was completely the wrong course of action, especially as the Canadian government hadn't taken on board what Gouzenko had told them and still considered the Soviet Union an ally.

Bill sprang into action. He ensured that the Royal Canadian Mounted Police took Gouzenko into protective custody while he organised the next steps. He got BSC agents to interview Gouzenko and find out all of the information that they could. Once they had everything they needed, Gouzenko and his wife were secretly moved to Camp X, where they were kept guarded.

Bill travelled back to New York and relayed the information to Britain across a secure communications link. Gouzenko had revealed a huge intelligence operation across the USA and Canada. The espionage activity was incredibly deep, and what Gouzenko revealed led to arrests of numerous spies as well as helping with deciphering coded messages. The defection of Gouzenko was a highly significant moment, in both a positive and negative way. While his defection offered a large amount of information to the British, Canadian, and US governments, it also ushered in the Cold War, and the defection of Gouzenko is often thought to be the official start of it. Gouzenko spoke to a man named, coincidentally, William Stevenson, who was writing a book about Bill Stephenson. He told Stevenson that he owed his life and the life of his children to Bill and wanted to be remembered to him. Stevenson informed Bill of this information when he saw him next, which drew a smile from the old spymaster.

Chapter 6: Post-War Life

Once the war was over, Bill and his wife Mary decided to live in semi-retirement. At 49, he was younger than most retirees, but he had the money to be able just to enjoy the time he had left. While he still had his business interests from before the war, he didn't really spend a great deal of time on them as before. His personal assistant controlled his business interests, just like she had done during the war, and this allowed Bill the opportunity to enjoy the fortune that he had managed to accrue. He also started to sell off some aspects that he wasn't that interested in. His shares in the film studio alone were sold for £380,000. One thing that came out after the war was that he had volunteered his services during the war. He had a significant income, and his businesses had actually benefited from the outbreak of war, and so he decided that he didn't need to be paid for what he was doing. He just wanted to help the war effort and so dedicated his time to the cause for free.

The war had had a profound effect on Bill. He felt completely disillusioned with the world at the end of the Second World War. He couldn't see why countries were still spying on each other and spending their time researching deadly weapons when they had just managed to escape a global catastrophe. It was something that bothered him for the rest of his life. It was a feeling that he shared with his friend Nöel Coward – both men felt that in 1945, the world should have become a kinder place.

Bill and Mary hosted many parties, and just like before, they included a wide range of people who were important in the world. The difference was that this time Bill wasn't collecting information; he was just enjoying their company. Bill and Mary had homes in Jamaica, New York, and Montreal and so were able to travel the world at a moment's notice. Bill had made friends with some moderately famous people during his career, including both Ian Fleming and Nöel Coward. His parties tended to include people of this ilk while also having people from high society attending as well.

By 1951, with Bill over the age of 50 and his body starting to slow down slightly, the Stephensons decided to sell their house in Jamaica and settle down in New York. The strain of travelling was starting to become too much, and they wanted to relax a little more as they got older. They bought an apartment that took up an entire floor. Such was the level of luxury they were living in that their downstairs neighbour was none other than Greta Garbo.

Despite being in semi-retirement, Bill still indulged in some work if something of interest came about. After settling down in New York, he was contacted by the premier of Newfoundland and asked to be the chairman of the Newfoundland and Labrador Corporation. His job was to entice new businesses and attempt to increase investment in the area. His ability at this job was incredible, although not surprising. Something that Bill had always been good at was making contacts. He used his large list of contacts to ensure that Newfoundland had more than enough new businesses and investment for the next four years. Despite his success, Bill resigned in 1952, telling the Newfoundland premier that he felt the job should be headed up by someone more local. The premier accepted his resignation reluctantly but thanked him for the fantastic job that he had done.

Around this time, he also used his contacts to bring a large hydro development to Labrador. He was the subject of a magazine piece because of this, in which his achievements in Newfoundland, although not what he had achieved during the war, were celebrated. Bill was called a great Canadian who had done a lot to help Canada start to achieve in line with its enormous potential.

Bill also had a part in the setting up of the World

Commerce Corporation. Based in New York, it allowed him to commit as much time as he wanted without having to worry about travel if there was a business emergency that he had to attend to. The WCC had a great deal of success but also had many failures, as well. It could most generously be described as a mixed bag. It contained several workers from both the BSC and the OSS. While at first glance this may seem like a good idea, the BSC and OSS agents had been trained in espionage and intelligence. Some of their skills translated to the business world well, but not all of them. Bill was also taking a back seat role. He felt that he had served his time; he had enough money to last the rest of his life, and he wanted just to enjoy himself.

It was obvious which areas in the WCC Bill had been involved in because these were the areas that tended to be successful. Bill used both his influence in the cement world and his ties to Jamaica to bring several cement companies to Jamaica. The governor of Jamaica had approached Bill for help with this, and he felt that he could help an old friend while at the same time using it to make his business more successful. Before the WCC set up a cement industry in Jamaica, they imported it. This was a lengthy, expensive, and highly inefficient method. This led to a £600,000 profit for the company, but more importantly to Bill, it had led to Jamaica saving £3,000,000 purely by making their cement domestically.

He continued to be involved in the Caribbean for a long time and dedicated a lot of his time to trying to improve the conditions in Jamaica and the surrounding countries.

Bill also dedicated his time to helping Canada. When the Manitoba Minister of Industry and Commerce approached him for help, it was Bill's contacts that allowed him to meet with a number of important captains of industry within New York. Bill also took on an honorary position within Manitoba's Economic Advisory Board. Bill's name being associated with Manitoba helped to deliver increased investment and drove more interest to the area. Even though he had worked under a cloak of secrecy during the war, the name of Bill Stephenson was still highly regarded in the business world. It allowed Manitoba to truly accelerate their growth at a rate they wouldn't have been capable of without Bill's help.

In the early 1960s, the Stephensons suffered a major blow to their life of retirement. Bill suffered a major stroke that left him with serious speech issues and limited his movement. Bill, being the fighter that he was, though, continued to work on improving himself. This was the push that Bill needed to take retiring seriously. Bill and his wife left New York forever and properly retired to Bermuda. Here he was able to relax properly, and the Stephensons cut themselves off from pretty much everyone. While no one knows for sure, it is suspected that Bill didn't want people to see him in the state he was in.

The stroke had made him a shadow of his former self, and Bill Stephenson was a proud man. He wanted people to remember him as the businessman and spy captain, not the stroke victim.

Despite suffering the stroke in the early 1960s, Bill still had plenty of life left in him. During the 1970s, he used what political power he had left to try and push for tidal power. He knew that fossil fuels wouldn't last forever and that they were slowly destroying the Earth. Therefore, he wanted to push for more renewable forms of energy. Even in the 1970s, Bill was a man way ahead of his time. By the 1970s, he was closer to the man he had been before the stroke, partly due to the excellent work of a British neurosurgeon who had been recommended to Bill by the author Roald Dahl. This meant that he had a lot more visitors to his Bermuda home.

Pauline McGibbon was one person who started to visit Bill every year. She was the lieutenant governor of Ontario and had visited Bermuda for a routine trip. When Bill heard she had come, he requested to see her. Once the two met, they instantly clicked on a personal level, and that was the start of her yearly visit to the Stephensons. It wasn't all pleasant, though; Mary, Bill's wife, had been diagnosed with terminal cancer.

Mary was unable to get out of bed at this point. Bill had a live-in nurse, Elizabeth Baptiste, who tended to Mary at all times. In 1977, Mary finally succumbed to her illness and died.

Elizabeth Baptiste remained on Bill's payroll to look after him. She and her son both lived in the Stephenson home in Bermuda. Bill was so grateful for everything that Elizabeth did for him and Mary that he eventually adopted her as his daughter.

Throughout Bill's time in Bermuda, he was still seen as an expert in the matters of intelligence. In fact, the sheer number of contacts that he had gathered over the years meant that he often knew information before it appeared in the news. He often sent telex messages to his friends around the world to inform them of items of interest.

The high regard that Bill was held in, combined with his high level of expertise, meant that as soon as he had recovered from his stroke and was able to communicate effectively, he had visits from people all around the world seeking his advice and help.

Bill was highly upset by the actions of Richard Nixon, and he felt that Canada could use this to finally take the position as the world's superpower that he felt they deserved. While Bill spent a lot of his time attempting to help the poorer countries of the world grow, he was still a patriot at heart. Bill was often referred to as 'The Quiet Canadian', and he felt that this was the best way to describe him. He even preferred this moniker to the awards that he had won from the American and British governments.

Bill had become quite paranoid by the time he moved to Bermuda. He knew that his influence on the Second World War had made him a marked man in certain quarters. This led to a great deal of worry and meant that when he visited Winnipeg one final time in 1980, he didn't let anyone know and didn't see any of his family members. His family believed it was because he wanted to keep a low profile. They were all under the impression that his Bermuda home was guarded by mounted police at all times. While Bill was worried about his safety, he hadn't quite gone to that extent. Whatever Bill's reasons, he left Winnipeg without seeing any of his relations.

Another reason that Bill didn't visit his relatives was because in all of the books written about him while he was alive, he had given false details. He fabricated a huge amount of his life, even going so far as to have a fake teacher be interviewed in order to give an insight into his school life. Bill desired to be able to write his own history. Whether it was out of ego or fear, the reason why went to the grave with him.

The only family member he had been in touch with in any way was his brother's wife, Lillian. His brother had died years before, so perhaps Bill felt that she was someone who could give him a link to his past life without having to worry about being in touch with other people whom he didn't want contact with, for whatever reason.

On the 31st of January, 1989, Bill Stephenson passed away. He was survived by his adopted daughter and her son,

Rhys. His body was buried in Bermuda, completely in secret and without any funeral.

Bill had told Elizabeth that he didn't want his death to be made known until after he was buried. Even in death, he was paranoid that someone might desecrate his corpse or his burial site if his death was made public knowledge. When Bill died, the media reported that he was the last remaining member of his family despite there being a significant number of relatives left living in Winnipeg.

Bill Stephenson was a man who dedicated his life to helping his country as well as the countries that took him in as one of their own. He made Britain the shining light of military intelligence. He helped to bring America up to a similar standard as the British. His birthplace of Canada received a number of his business interests to help their economy. Even Jamaica, where he had lived for several years, he spent time helping them to become more self-sufficient. Bill Stephenson was a patriot, but he was also a man who felt that the whole world needed help, not just the country where he was born.

Chapter 7: Bill's Secret Agents

One of the biggest aspects of how Bill had conducted the intelligence aspect of the war was how he had brought in agents to do specific jobs. It came out after the war that there had been a range of agents who were either famous or who had a large impact on the war without being well known. It was the modus operandi of Bill and the BSC. They brought in people who had specific skills to carry out specific tasks. This is part of what made the BSC so effective. They didn't attempt to shoehorn people into jobs that didn't suit them. If there were a job that needed to be carried out, then the right person would be recruited and trained to carry it out effectively.

What isn't well known about the BSC is that at times Bill would fund it out of his own pocket. Funding for the intelligence agency wasn't seen as a top priority to the higher-ups within the British government, and as the organisation grew, so did the costs. While Bill was an independently wealthy man and could happily work without a salary, as he did, he knew that not all of his agents were in the same situation. So, when the funding to pay the salaries of his agents wasn't forthcoming, Bill would cover the costs. He knew the importance of the BSC to the war effort, so he knew that it couldn't afford to have agents who didn't feel wanted and respected. Overall, the BSC cost Bill Stephenson in the region of $3,000,000, which would be worth around $42,000,000 today. Because Bill Stephenson valued his agents so much, their stories are intertwined with his own and are almost as important as Bill's own story.

Here, we will cover the impact of some of the agents who had a large impact on Bill's legacy but weren't a huge part of his life as a whole. His legacy as the head of the BSC and to some people, the father of modern espionage, wouldn't be what it is without the hard work and dedication of these secret agents.

Cynthia

Cynthia first drew the attention of the BSC when she was living in South America with her husband. She started to write under an assumed name, Elizabeth Thomas and carried out fifth column activities in favour of the British war effort. The propaganda that she had been creating was aimed at creating more sympathy for the British and removing the anti-British feeling that pervaded the Americas at the time. The BSC heard about her activities and got her to New York to meet with Bill. It was here that he found out who she really was. She was Elizabeth Pack, the daughter of a US veteran. She had married quite young to an older man, Arthur Pack.

Bill found out that she had carried out some espionage work in Poland earlier in the war. She had started a relationship with a Polish aide and used that to get as much information as possible. It was from here that she found out information about the ENIGMA machine and helped to smuggle the secrets back to Britain. While she hadn't been a highly important part of cracking the ENIGMA code, her help was undoubtedly helpful.

Bill was impressed with his latest recruit and gave her the codename Cynthia. Once she had her codename, she was given her first assignment. She was sent to talk to a former friend of hers who worked at the Italian embassy. She found out information from this that led to the capture of Italian ciphers.

In May of 1941, Cynthia's most famous exploits were carried out. As mentioned earlier in Bill's story, Cynthia carried out an intelligence mission at the French Vichy embassy. Cynthia pretended to be an American journalist. From here, she asked the press attaché to organise an interview with the French Vichy ambassador. The attaché was a man named Charles Brousse. He organised the interview for Cynthia, but she noted that he could be the entry point for her into the embassy. She managed this by embarking on an affair with Brousse.

Through her affair, she managed to find out a great deal of information, but the most important information she found out was that Brousse didn't like either the ambassador or the French Vichy prime minister. Brousse was fervently anti-British, which led to Cynthia being extremely upfront about her American heritage. She made sure that she memorised everything that was said at dinners where she was invited, but she also had to be careful when conducting her affair with Charles because he was already married. Brousse's anger towards the embassy and Prime Minister was severely ramped up when he found out that he had the choice of being sent back to Vichy or take a job within the embassy with lower pay and lower prestige.

Cynthia knew that this was her opportunity to really get some intelligence that would be useful for the BSC. She also knew that Brousse hating the British meant that she would have to lie to him. She told Brousse that she was an American agent and started to work at convincing him that helping her cause would be the best way to help France. She told him that the Nazis were not the people to help France. Despite his thoughts that the Nazis were the least bad option for the people to get help from, Brousse went along with the woman who had been sharing his bed for so long. What helped in this situation was that he trusted her a lot more than he trusted the openly Nazi-sympathizing French Vichy prime minister. Brousse decided to believe Cynthia when she told him that he would be behaving in a patriotic manner, and he started passing on everything that he physically could.

The two started taking slight risks, which came to a head when they were caught in the offices of the embassy at night. Thinking quickly, Cynthia swiftly removed her clothes to make it look like they were involved in a late night tryst. The guard bought the deception and left them to it.

By March of 1942, Cynthia had got herself well into the embassy operation, but the BSC gave her a job that she felt was almost impossible. Bill Stephenson asked her to ascertain the Vichy French naval ciphers. The Americans had officially become part of the war by this point, and the British and Americans were planning to invade North Africa. Therefore, they needed to be able to find out exactly where the French naval fleet would be and what kind of ships they had. Cynthia told Bill that she would do her best, but she didn't hold out much hope of completing the mission.

By the time she had got back to Washington, she had devised a plan. Before she carried out the plan she attempted to gain access to the codes purely by asking. She spoke to the two men who had access to the codes and tried to convince them that it would be better for France if they allowed the codes to fall into the hands of the Americans. She had no luck with this line of reasoning and so decided to go ahead with her plan.

She told Charles that they should talk to the guard who had caught them before and ask him if he could set it up so they could make regular clandestine meetings. The guard agreed, and from then on the couple would meet in the embassy most evenings. This allowed them a way to get into the embassy without arousing any suspicion.

While this was going on, they discovered where the cipher codes were hidden and engaged the services of a noted safecracker. One night during one of their trysts, they snuck the safecracker into the embassy and made their way to the code room. Once inside, the safecracker managed to get into the safe. By 1 a.m., the codes had made their way to an agent stationed outside, by 4 a.m., the codes had been copied and returned to the safe.

Cynthia had pulled off a job that she once thought impossible. The intelligence that she had managed to gather was of the highest importance and was of great help to the Allied war effort.

She continued to work for the BSC until the end of the war. After the war ended, her husband, Arthur, killed himself. She hadn't loved him for a long time but was still noticeably distraught by his suicide. She ended up marrying Charles Brousse and living in France until her death from cancer in 1963. Cynthia had been one of Bill's most trusted agents and had used her supreme intelligence and feminine charms to pull off some of the most difficult missions of the war.

In some quarters, the existence of Cynthia was disputed. However, the fact that she ended up married to Charles Brousse, something that is verifiable and therefore completely factual, combined with several eye witness accounts who both met her and had knowledge of the work she carried out, means that this particular claim is one of two things. It could be yet another smear intended to besmirch the name of Bill Stephenson, or it could just be that when it comes to the world of military intelligence, there is a lot of smoke-and-mirrors to try to keep things hidden.

Marion de Chastelain

Marion was first introduced to the BSC in November of 1940. Her husband had been involved in espionage at an earlier juncture in the war, and so when she travelled to New York to visit her mother, the BSC decided to make contact and attempt to bring her into the fold. She intended to stay in New York only for a short time initially, but her mother became sick, and so her stay was lengthened. When the BSC approached her and asked her to do her bit for king and country, Marion decided to stay close to her mother and join the BSC.

Because of the work her husband had carried out, the interview that Marion had to complete was extremely simple. A lot of British intelligence workers during the Second World War tended to be family members of people already involved in espionage, purely because it made it a much easier transition. They were already used to the way it worked and could fall into the work a lot easier.

It only took two weeks for Bill to notice that Marion was excellent at her job. He decided to move her up to a more important role. As Marion was fluent in French, Bill knew that she was valuable, but her skills at carrying out her job meant that she stood out even more.

One of the first major jobs that Marion took on was working as the handler for Cynthia. She met up with her in Washington to collect the information that she had managed to acquire. Marion was skilled at ensuring they didn't arouse suspicion. Each time the two women met, Marion made sure that it was in a different place. She also took different routes to get to where she needed to be. Marion was an absolute professional, and it made sense why Bill had chosen her.

As well as collecting the information from Cynthia, Marion also acted almost as an agony aunt. She listened to the problems that Cynthia was having and noticed when she was becoming too tired. Marion always got along well with Cynthia although after the job at the Vichy French embassy was over, the two women never had any contact again.

Marion didn't just work as Cynthia's handler; she also worked as a cipher clerk directly under Bill. Marion was one of just three people, one of whom was Bill, who had access to a safe containing the equipment for decoding messages. She was an integral part of Bill's inner sanctum. Marion ensured that all of the messages that came into the BSC were instantly decoded and then sent directly to Bill. There was no in-between – they went straight from Marion to Bill. That's not to say that Bill was the only person who read them. His personal secretary most likely had access to the messages as well, but Bill trusted her completely.

One very difficult decision that Marion had to deal with was some of the fifth column activity that the BSC carried out. Her father worked for Standard Oil, and the BSC had created and spread a pamphlet that explained how several large American companies, one of which was Standard Oil, had subsidiaries abroad, and those smaller subsidiaries were helping the Nazi war effort. This was obviously an attempt to stop the American people using products from these companies, and the MD of Standard Oil was particularly angry about it. Marion never told her father what she knew despite there being a $50,000 reward on offer to anyone who could tell Standard Oil who had created the pamphlet. Marion knew that her country came first even though the money would have been worth a huge amount at the time.

Marion was also one of the first lines of defence when it came to deflecting visitors. A great number of people wanted to see Bill, but there were very few who had the clearance to see him. Even for those who had the clearance, Bill sometimes left strict instructions that he was to be left alone. One of the few people who were allowed to see Bill was Bill Donovan. Marion said that he was a frequent visitor to the BSC offices.

During 1941, it became apparent to the BSC that the Japanese were extremely unlikely to successfully negotiate with the Americans. Given this, Bill and Bill Donovan were suspicious about what the Japanese would do. Marion was aware of this as she saw and heard what Bill was saying. While she wasn't aware of Bill knowing any specific dates about the Pearl Harbor attack, she felt that Bill knew that it was coming, but Roosevelt either didn't get his warnings in time or didn't take any notice of them.

By 1943, Marion decided that she wanted to return home to England. Bill was extremely sad to see her go and managed to convince her to carry on her espionage work when she returned home. He knew that losing Marion would be a blow to the work the BSC had carried out. When she returned, she started working for Section 5 of MI6. Here, she worked on decoded messages. She had to deal with a large number of messages each day and found the work a lot duller than what she had done with the BSC in New York.

During this time, Marion's husband was taken prisoner while on a mission in Romania, and she didn't see him again until 1944 when he was released. This led to several problems for Marion once the war had finished as she and her husband weren't allowed back into Romania at any point because of the level of intelligence that her husband had picked up.

Once the war was over, Marion remained close friends with Bill and his wife and visited them many times. She visited them in New York before Bill's stroke and travelled to Bermuda to see them after Bill retired completely.

Marion continued to visit Bill right up to his death and was one of two people who knew him and his work best during his wartime years. She was one of his most trusted agents, which is shown by how he ensured that she got a job with MI6 when she returned to England.

Joan Bright Astley

A lot of the work that Bill carried out during the war is lost to the sands of time. While his work in the Americas is generally well documented, what he did in Europe is relatively unknown. During the war, he made a great number of trips back to Europe, both documented and undocumented, but there was one person who he used as a contact when in London: Joan Bright Astley.

Joan had worked several jobs within the government

before the war broke out. She started her career working in the English Foreign Office based in Mexico. By 1938, she was working in the anti-tank unit of the Territorial Army. When war broke out, she was headhunted by the military and started working in Section D. It was through this that she met several people involved in the intelligence aspects of the war. Bill Stephenson was one of them.

She knew that Bill had been a significant influence on Bill Donovan. She wrote a book about her wartime experiences and said that Bill had convinced Donovan that the US needed to start taking steps in the intelligence business, regardless of whether they were going to join the war or not.

Astley was slightly different in her approach to the secrecy of espionage. Whether this was a cover to maintain the secrets of wartime intelligence or not isn't known, but she routinely refused to use the word spying and insisted on calling it the service. She also divulged that at times, Winston Churchill didn't like using the information that had been gathered by the BSC. He felt like it was cheating, and he wanted to win the war fair and square.

However, despite this, she spoke of Bill Stephenson with nothing but warmth. She felt it was wrong how British intelligence never countered some of the smears that that appeared about Bill in the media and that he had played a vital role in the allies winning the war.

While Joan Bright Astley never directly worked for the BSC, she was still someone that Bill knew well and regarded as a friend. She visited the Stephensons in Bermuda quite regularly and was a friend of Bill's wife, Mary, as well as Bill. She knew that the man known as Intrepid was an excellent intelligence agent and had helped to turn the tide of the war the way of the Allies. Joan Bright Astley may never have been an agent of Bill Stephenson's, but she knew him better than most people.

Roald Dahl

Roald Dahl is one of the most surprising names on the list of agents that Bill Stephenson brought into the BSC, having the honour of being one of the most beloved children's authors of all time. His body of work stands up to that of almost any writer in the world, but on top of this, he was also a fighter pilot and spy during the Second World War. It was after a crash landing where Dahl suffered a wide range of injuries – including a life-threatening skull fracture – that he moved to Washington to work as an assistant air attaché at the British Embassy.

When questioned, Dahl was actually quite cagey about how he became one of Bill Stephenson's agents, but what is known is that he was a regular visitor to the White House. His writing was a particular favourite of Eleanor Roosevelt's, and that allowed him access to the president that other people may not have been able to get. Therefore, Bill Stephenson knew that getting Dahl onside was important in regards to keeping Roosevelt and Churchill on speaking terms.

As Dahl was friends with both men, it allowed Bill to transfer information between the two of them using a friendly face. It was an ingenious plan that led to the relationship between Roosevelt and Churchill being far smoother than many expected.

Dahl was a regular visitor to the BSC offices and recalled that Bill very rarely interacted with the staff who weren't of direct importance to him. This meant that very few people really knew Bill in an agency of well over a thousand people – this most likely equated to less than 30 people who really knew Bill and what he did during the war. Dahl felt that he was one of the people who ended up knowing Bill well.

Once Dahl was actually signed up to work with the BSC, it was over a year before he met Bill Stephenson. Once he did, the two got on famously. Dahl's main contribution to the war effort, apart from keeping Roosevelt and Churchill on speaking terms, was to steal information from as many places as possible. As the air attaché, he got to see a wide range of private information. One of his most prominent missions was to get hold of a paper by Vice President Henry Wallace. In the paper, it outlined a number of plans to limit the British influence in the post-war world. Dahl got in touch with a contact at the BSC and had the paper copied and sent over to Churchill. He was furious when he found out, and there are long-standing rumours that the BSC and Bill had a part to play in the removal of Wallace for the 1944 election.

By 1943, Dahl was working solely for the BSC and was used as a go-between for American and British agents. Part of this was due to his close friendship with Roosevelt, which meant that Dahl had easy access to the highest point of American democracy. He would ask questions in an informal setting but would then pass on the information to Bill when he returned.

One aspect that Dahl found interesting was how Bill managed to entice him further into the espionage game. Dahl had been sacked as the air attaché for insulting some air marshals. Dahl got word to Bill that he had been sent home because of misconduct. Bill told him not to worry about it and to go and see a man within the BSC when he could. Once there, Dahl was told that he would be returned to Washington as a Wing Commander and would be working directly for Bill. Dahl was impressed by the power that Bill had.

Dahl was asked by Bill to write the history of the BSC, the book that was to become the intelligence bible, but Dahl tried and struggled to do it. He told Bill that he was a fiction writer and the book really needed to be written by a historian. Bill told him not to worry and commissioned someone else to carry out the work.

Dahl remained friends with Bill after the war, but his opinion of him was a strange one. On the one hand, he felt that Bill was a brilliant man who knew a great deal about the world of business and intelligence. But on the other, he felt that he wasn't particularly interesting when outside of those worlds. He said that Bill was an uncultured man who offered very little in the way of conversation. He felt that part of this could have been due to his upbringing, but also because he was such a secretive man.

Dahl was still impressed by the work that Bill had carried out, and he said that Bill had told him that the achievement he was most proud of during the war was negotiating the loan of destroyers early on in his BSC career.

The two men got on well, even though Dahl felt Bill was uncultured, and he said that Bill was one of the only men involved in intelligence who remained faithful to his wife throughout. They continued to exchange telegrams and telex messages, and Dahl even visited Bill in Bermuda. Bill Stephenson was a very secretive man, but Roald Dahl was also quite secretive and elusive when it came to revealing information about Bill Stephenson.

Grace Garner

Grace Garner was possibly the single most important

person to Bill Stephenson in relation to his job as head of BSC. She was his head secretary for the entire time the BSC was running, and whenever anyone needed to see Bill, they had to go through her first. Grace had worked for Bill and the BSC since before the move to Rockefeller Center. She knew Bill from the very start and grew to be his most trusted employee even though she wasn't an agent.

According to Grace Garner, most of the early recruiting for the BSC was carried out by Thomas Drew-Brook. This was because he was a man whom Bill trusted, but he was also a man who had a range of different skills that he had picked up from his time as a fighter pilot. Drew-Brook and his wife would help to bring the new recruits over and then ship them off to Camp X as soon as possible.

Drew-Brook would sort out several details for the new recruits. If they weren't already settled in the area, he would ensure that they had flats to live in. He also put forward the idea of using newspaper advertisements to recruit more women to the operation.

Garner kept her true position hidden throughout the war. She knew that Bill was an important person in British intelligence. She saw first-hand the majority of the work that passed through his office, so she was well aware of the importance of keeping a low profile. If she were ever asked what her job was, she would claim that she worked for the British Purchasing Commission. This wasn't technically a lie as she had started out there before the BSC absorbed it. The demands of her job as Bill's head secretary meant that Grace didn't really have a lot of time for a social life, this meant that on the whole she was very rarely asked what her job was.

Garner was there for all of the early troubles that the BSC had. When Bill was attempting to negotiate more destroyers for the British Navy. When the fifth column activities were being ramped up to try to turn the tide of American isolationism. She knew the difficulties that Bill faced but did her best to make sure that everything was organised for him.

Garner said that the only real security precaution for the women working in the BSC offices was that they couldn't have American boyfriends. This was so that they didn't become compromised as at the time the Americans weren't on board with the war. She told of one woman having to resign because she had fallen in love with a US marine and ended up marrying him.

She was shocked that the BSC managed to remain out of sight of American eyes for so long. They operated out in the open so much but, partly because the Americans didn't have a truly dedicated intelligence service of their own, they didn't manage to find out about it. This was partly because they wouldn't have known the signs to look out for. She was especially shocked because there was a watch company on the floor above them and the BSC workers got into a running battle with the watch company workers over the use of the elevators. Because so many of the BSC agents, clerks, and secretaries were Canadian, it should have aroused suspicion, in Garner's opinion. It never did, though.

One piece of intelligence work that Garner did carry out was to identify a Swedish agent who was loitering in the foyer of Rockefeller Center. This was not long after the BSC had been involved with the stopping of a Swedish supply to the Germans. Bill had spotted him as he entered the building but fortunately managed to get out and enter through another entrance before he was spotted himself. He instantly told Garner to get in touch with Hall, who was a New York Private Detective. She attempted to get in touch with him but couldn't get hold of him at all. She decided that there was no time to lose and so went down to the foyer herself. She knew that the Swedish agent wouldn't know who she was, so she was able to get a good look at him without drawing attention to herself.

Once she had spotted someone who she felt looked suspicious loitering around and who hadn't been seen in the area before, she got a good look at him and returned upstairs to Bill. Here she described the man to him, and Bill knew right away that he had been correct. He instantly sent a telegram informing the right people that the Swedish were possibly onto them and they needed to be more careful than usual.

Garner brought some of the girls in the local lingerie shop on board as well. Because there was a girl from the British

Embassy who would use the girls in the lingerie shop to wrap up the contents of the diplomatic bag, the BSC tasked them with taking any important documents to get copied before they were wrapped up. They would do this by distracting the girl from the embassy with talk about the latest lines that were released.

Grace would usually stay away from the espionage side of things, though her main job was to arrange all of Bill's appointments. She knew who should be sent up to see him instantly and who should always be put off from seeing him. She also had to arrange his calendar to make sure that he could fit in appointments around his visits to different sites around the world. Bill didn't carry out all of his work in just one place. He travelled to a wide range of different places to ensure that the BSC intelligence operation was running smoothly in every location. It was Garner who ensured that his calendar was organised correctly, and he had as few double bookings as possible.

Garner was another who was annoyed at the attempt to smear Bill's name in the media after his death. An article in a British newspaper claimed that there was no evidence that Bill had ever met, let alone ever had anything to do with, Lord Beaverbrook and, more shockingly, Winston Churchill. This is something that Garner categorically denied as untrue. Beaverbrook was someone whom Bill met with frequently.

Not only were they both Canadian, but they were also in the same line of business. She feels that even if Bill had never got into intelligence, he would still have been an associate of Lord Beaverbrook. The Churchill claim she also dismissed as a smear, possibly borne of a desire from the home office to keep as many secrets as possible, or possibly from bitterness from people whom Bill hadn't allowed into his inner circle during the war.

She notes that despite Bill doing a lot of good and being highly thought of by a large number of people, it is important to realise that he also made enemies. Not everyone was allowed to carry out as much as they would have liked during the war, and Bill could also be quite an intimidating man if someone crossed him. This combined with his putting the noses of some important people out of joint meant that there would be some people who couldn't miss the opportunity to smear his name.

Bill had several different secretaries who worked for him; the majority would work shifts. Grace Garner was different, however. As she was his head secretary and the one that he trusted the most, she would start at 7 a.m. and finish at 8 p.m. every day. This meant that she was there for the majority of the working day. She was also over the switchboard operators for the BSC. While the BSC itself didn't have a phone number, because Bill had started out as the head of Passport Control, the phone number for there would be directed straight to the

BSC offices. From here, Garner would decide which messages were most urgent for Bill and put them in the right order for him to see.

Garner was another employee of the BSC who was aware of the existence of Cynthia. Garner wasn't just aware of Cynthia, but she was there when Bill brought in Marion de Chastelain to act as her handler. While Garner never actually met with Cynthia herself, she knew that Marion had on a number of occasions. She knew that Marion was extremely trustworthy, and she also knew that Bill had tasked her with handling Cynthia. This was enough for Garner to say that Cynthia was 100% an agent who worked for the BSC.

Garner was also around when Roald Dahl was brought on board. According to Garner, Dahl had carried out minor intelligence for the BSC early on in the war but didn't come on board officially until 1943. Here he worked as Bill's personal assistant for a while before he was moved back to Washington to work as a liaison at that end for a while.

Garner also offered some insight into the working tension that built up between the BSC and the FBI. It's known that by the early 1940s, Hoover and the FBI were not happy that the BSC were carrying out their work to such a great extent in the USA. A lot of this was due to the stirring carried out by Adolf Berle, the Assistant Secretary of State. She wasn't sure if the story of a BSC agent attempting to dig up some dirt on Berle were true or not. She knew that he had been hurried over the border to Canada as soon as it appeared the FBI was onto what he was doing. What she didn't know was if the agent had been doing it or if an FBI agent had been planted to make it seem like he was doing it. She did say that it wouldn't surprise her if he had done it, but there were a lot of rumours flying around at the time and no one, apart from Bill Stephenson and the agent in question, was completely aware of the facts.

While it is claimed that Bill made over 40 trips back to Europe during his time as the head of the BSC, Garner feels that this number is a lot less. She feels that it would be closer to 20 at the most. This is due to the complex nature of the trip and because of the danger to Bill himself if it got out that he was travelling. Of course, it is possible that Bill made secret trips to Europe without Garner's knowledge, especially as he had to travel from Canada to get there. It would have been easy for him to make a trip to Canada and secretly travel to Europe without telling her in order to minimise risk.

Garner said that she only ever upset Bill once during her time as his head secretary. Most of the agents and operations had codenames. When they came through via telegram, there would often be a codename included in the message. One time she mentioned that the codename for someone was funny and was greeted by a deathly silence from Bill. She knew right away that she had overstepped the mark and made sure never to do so again. As many people have mentioned, Bill took his business very seriously, and he saw the BSC as his business. This meant that he had no time for humour, especially about something like codenames that had to be protected at all costs.

There were also several office moves that happened to the BSC during the course of their lifespan. Garner was there for them all. The one that she remembers most is when they took over the Japanese consulate. This was after the Pearl Harbor bombings when it was made clear that the consulate was no longer welcome in the USA. Within two days of the bombings, Bill had made the consulate the new office for the BSC. As the consulate was in the same building as where they were already based, they didn't lose their old offices – they simply incorporated another floor. This was important to Bill as the BSC was expanding constantly and he knew that they would need a great deal of space to carry out their work efficiently. This left them with both the 38th and 35th floor of Rockefeller Center. Part of the reason that they kept their old offices as well was that they had many machines already installed there, and it wouldn't have been time or cost effective to move them, as well.

Garner was also against a large amount of literature that came out over the years about Bill. She also felt that there was a lot out there that diminished the reputation that Bill had worked for his entire life. She did feel that some of the more frequent errors surrounding Bill's life, mainly based around his childhood, were planted by Bill himself. He had always wanted to keep his childhood a secret, for whatever reason, and so when given the opportunity, he spread untruths.

She also had a lot of information about some of the fifth column activities of the BSC. The pamphlet that they created that caused such a storm with Standard Oil was entitled *The Uncensored Story of How Your Dimes And Quarters Pay For Hitler's War*. Inside, it included a range of profiles of North American businesses that were making a profit from working with the Nazis. Bill had never been shy of making money from the war – a range of his businesses were specifically geared towards it. However, he had never profited from Nazi money. All of his businesses solely worked for Allied needs. This move by some American companies was something he felt strongly about, so he pressed ahead as firmly as he could to use it to help turn the tide of public opinion away from American isolationism.

There was also a huge amount of BSC fifth column activity in South America. This was an area that had previously had a lot of pro-British feeling, but once war broke out and Britain withdrew their funds from South America, it initiated a lot of anti-British feeling. The BSC used several ways to turn public opinion around. It wasn't so much turning them pro-British, rather it was more a case of turning them anti-Nazi. South America was seen as something of a Nazi stronghold. The activity worked in some parts, but there were areas that it wasn't as successful, hence why a lot of prominent Nazis fled to South America after the war.

One of the major fifth column activities that Garner had information about was the production of a fake map of South America. It showed the proposed takeover that the Nazis had planned for the area. It was distributed in the USA to try to induce panic amongst the populace. A lot of the work undertaken by the BSC was working, but before it had a chance to fully take hold, the Pearl Harbor attacks took place.

Pat Bayly

Pat Bayly was quite possibly the most secretive member of the BSC. There is very little mention of Bayly in terms of wartime activity with the BSC anywhere. It is surprising in a way because Bayly was actually second-in-command to Bill Stephenson for the majority of the war.

Bayly had been a professor at the University of Toronto before the war broke out. He had originally been a lawyer, but he hated the job so went back to university to study engineering. It was here that he showed a prodigious degree of talent, and in an incredibly rare situation, he was employed to teach the fourth year of the degree while he was still a third-year student. It caused a slightly troublesome situation when it was time for him to graduate, but eventually, the governors decided that he could just give himself an A. He continued to work teaching at the university for the remainder of the 1930s.

He had also been involved with several radio stations before he became a lawyer. This was where he had developed a lot of his electrical engineering skills. His knowledge of radio broadcasts was second-to-none.

Once war broke out, he started working on various jobs in the background for the Canadian war effort. He was approached by Thomas Drew-Brook to join the BSC. Bill had tasked him with finding the best people for the BSC, and his research had drawn him to Bayly.

In November of 1941, Bayly travelled to Britain to learn about how their communications worked. His background in engineering combined with his career in radio meant that Drew-Brook knew that he would be perfect to work in the communications department of the fledgling intelligence agency. While he was there, he actually found himself disappointed with the personnel file that the British held on him. He saw the file on the desk of Stewart Menzies while he was waiting to see him and so had a look through. He found that they had been impressed by the school that he had gone to rather than the skills that he possessed. This was something that really made him feel let down, but he still intended to do the job well as he wanted to be a part of the war effort.

Bayly found that the British were incredibly behind in the field of communication. It became clear to him why Bill had worked so hard to make him part of his team. He wanted to bring the British communication up to date. He made the point that the British radios only had a range of 15 miles, yet the German tanks could travel at 30mph and so could make up 15 miles in just half an hour.

After signing the official secrets act and getting up to speed with British communication and ciphers, he travelled to meet with Bill in New York. By the time he got there, he knew that his potential mission would have to change slightly. He arrived on the 7th of December, just as the Pearl Harbor attacks were taking place. He knew there would be a change of plans.

When he got there, he told Bill that they needed to stop using the telephone. The security on telephones at that time was very poor, and so Bayly said that using a teleprinter and one-time pads was a much more secure way of working.

As the Americans had just joined the war, Bill invited them to join in with the standard security checks for Bayly. The FBI brought in the Royal Canadian Mounted Police, which made sense as Bayly was Canadian. The Mountie that they sent caused some problems with Bayly as he kept saying that he knew him from somewhere. This caused a panic within the FBI as they thought the only way a Mountie could know him was from his being involved with criminality. As it turned out, the Mountie's mother had been Bayly's music teacher, which significantly lowered the tension.

When Bayly first started with the BSC, they were using the FBI communication lines. This was soon stopped as J Edgar Hoover wasn't happy with how this made the USA look. They couldn't use the British embassy channel because they were untrustworthy, so it was all down to Bayly to set up new, trustworthy communication channels. Bayly organised the purchase of a Western Union system called the *telekrypton*. He improved on this system and started to expand it across the whole BSC network. Bayly ended up working in a range of places on improving communication and training how to use it. He was a vital piece of the cog in Washington, in London, and at Camp X.

It's difficult to pinpoint exactly what Bayly did for the BSC in terms of work because he is mentioned so sparingly. However, it is safe to assume that he had some hand in the workings of the fifth column radio station that the BSC ran for a short while in the USA.

Bayly himself said that part of the reason he ended up so high in the BSC was that Bill trusted him. Bill didn't trust British people that much, but as Bayly was a fellow Canadian, Bill took him into his trust. The communication network that Bayly set up was vital to the BSC's cause, which could be why Bayly eventually became known as their best-kept secret.

The Legacy of Intrepid

Bill Stephenson lived an inspiring, colourful life characterised by determination, hard work, and a loyalty that few men could boast of. From his humble and troubled beginnings in a dreary Winnipeg town to the accolades that afforded him his fortune and the prestige that he is still known for today, Bill Stephenson's life story is nothing short of a Hollywood tale that is yet to be told.

He was a remarkable individual whose fortitude played a major role in British and American history, and without Stephenson's efforts, many aspects of the Second World War could potentially have played out much differently.

Although he eventually referred to his war efforts as 'eighty per cent paperwork', this was merely Stephenson's modesty and lack of individualism once again coming into play. Likewise, he continually praised the BSC for their invaluable assistance, and history has shown us that perhaps

Stephenson's tale would indeed be less extravagant without their input.

Whether through business or espionage, Bill Stephenson always excelled. He remains a hero and a figure of inspiration to many, and unlike many of his lesser-known counterparts, his legacy has not diminished as time has passed by. The man known as Intrepid will remain one of the unsung heroes of the Second World War as long as accounts of his extraordinary life exist.

About Ethan Quinn

Ethan Quinn lives in the beautifully rural county of Herefordshire with his wife and child. In his spare time, he enjoys many different activities, such as walking, bouldering, and playing the traditional English sport of cricket.

Ethan has always been fascinated with people and the stories that they can tell. He believes that people are the most creative, unique, and surprising things on this planet, and some are more extraordinary than others. He strives to find out what drives these exceptional human beings to become what they are and do what they do, which is not always for good!

Ethan has a background in writing, and in 2017 he decided to follow his passion to write in the True Crime Espionage area about the incredible humans that become spies.

When writing he always tries to concentrate on the truth, and highlights what makes these people truly remarkable. This is done with complete honesty and attempting to understand their point of view because as mentioned earlier, these unique individuals didn't always stay within the law.

For more information about the author and his latest releases please visit Ethan Quinn's website:

WWW.ETHANQUINNBOOKS.COM

More Books by Ethan Quinn

Many terms were bestowed upon the mysterious Fritz Duquesne throughout his colourful life, but perhaps the most fitting ever attributed to him was: **"The most dangerous prisoner to have ever lived."**

Fritz Duquesne was a Boer War warrior-turned-spy who vowed revenge against the nation which took from him those he held dear. This lead to his own enrolment in the military of whichever side fought opposite the British forces.

Through complex prison escapes, destructive acts of sabotage, and heroic feats which are even too farfetched for fiction, Fritz Duquesne exacted revenge in the most daring, unbelievable, and all-round theatrical manner possible.

Fritz assumed many different identities and he ultimately became responsible for the largest espionage ring ever uncovered in the United States.

Known as Fritz to his German spy-handlers and Zig-Zag to the British secret service, Eddie Chapman was a man of many faces. While his early life was rife with petty crime, gang activity and a dishonourable discharge from the British military, Chapman's unique skills were eventually sought out by Nazi Germany, and after convincing them he could use his criminal contacts to sabotage the English forces, he was quickly recruited.

But Chapman's loyalty to his country knew no limits. A talented, handsome, and reckless Englishman, Chapman was a traitor on the surface but a fearless patriot on the inside. After cracking Germany's military code, the British sought Chapman for their own affairs, and Chapman was happy to oblige.

Eventually being awarded the prestigious Nazi Iron Cross for services to Germany while acting as a double agent for Britain, Chapman's espionage efforts involved masterful deceit and feats which few men alive could ever boast of.

Eddie Chapman's life story is an unbelievable journey of crime, jail-breaks, treachery, and love. He was responsible for saving countless lives during his career, **cementing himself as the ultimate double agent during World War II.**

ETHAN QUINN

Free Espionage Audiobook

If you are interested in reading another unbelievable story of espionage, then please follow the link to download a **FREE** copy of Iron Spy.

WWW.ETHANQUINNBOOKS.COM/FREE-AUDIOBOOK

"Another true tale of little known 'derring - do' by Ethan. A very insightful read of the life of an oft flawed character who demonstrated steely heroism during the Second World War - masterful!" **K.E. Fellows**

"The amazing story of Eddie Chapman until now has been a long lost secret within 20th century wartime history. A great piece of writing from Ethan Quinn to bring this important piece of history to life." **J Thomas**

"...Here's another brilliant double agent story that'll have you hooked from beginning to end. A must read!" **H. Davies**

"Another fantastic biography from Ethan Quinn. This real life story of Eddie Chapman will have you gripped and not wanting to put it down. You won't believe this really happened." **G. Probert**

WWW.ETHANQUINNBOOKS.COM/FREE-AUDIOBOOK

Printed in Great Britain
by Amazon